Work from Home Headhunter

10-Week Guide to Six-Figure Success

Diane O'Brien

DEDICATION

I dedicate this book to all the Moms out there looking to be a better example to their own kids. The working Moms, the stay-at-home Moms, the something in between Moms! We all are doing the best we can to give our family the most ideal life possible.

I also dedicate this book to all the young women college students that I hope can be empowered by books like this. There are lots of paths to make your dreams come true. I hope you find the women mentors in your life who will support you, and help you become the woman you want to be!

Finally, I dedicate this book to all the "Headhunting Housewives" out there acting as great 'change agents' in people lives, moving people from their current job to a better job! It's a unique career and I have the utmost respect for the women who can sustain in this competitive industry, especially while keeping their family as top priority!

Diane O'Brien

Table of Contents

Chapter 2- The Clients & The Job Order   Page 67

Week 2:

Introduction: Work from Home Headhunter

Why Headhunting

It's no secret that women everywhere dream of finding a way to work from home. Google reports that there are 1.5 million searches per month on the words "work from home." Radio stations report being bombarded by calls during any segment relating to "Money for Moms," according to Tory Johnson, Good Morning America's workplace contributor and New York Times best-selling coauthor of the book, "*Will Work from Home: Earn the Cash—Without the Commute.*" The book "*Undress for Success*" points out that just one company that advertises 'work at home positions' receives over 150 thousand applicants per year. Americans are hungry for new and innovative ways to work from home. In an ideal world, women could raise their kids (with the help of a nanny) and still make a corporate income, all from home base. The five million stay-at-home moms in this country seem to be constantly searching for ways to make money from home, as well as many of the sixty-three million women currently chained to an office, wishing for a way to be free.

For most women, how to go about attaining a dream lifestyle that would allow them to successfully balance work and home life seems to be an unfathomable mystery. Worse yet, most books on "work from home" topics focus on lower-level jobs that most soccer moms would not be proud to discuss at a cocktail party or charity event, much less actually do on a daily basis. Data processing, customer service, envelope stuffing, virtual assistant work, and the like, may be a good fit for the non-degreed moms looking for a second income, but not so much for the college-educated woman who has chosen to leave a corporate job behind to be with her kids. Nor would those types of stay-at-home jobs attract women still at the office, or college women looking for a hot new career choice that will transition to home when needed.

In fact, most of America has not been properly introduced to this mysterious, secretive, lucrative career choice. Women can do it from home, on their own time, and make six figures while talking on the phone...and no, it's not phone sex! It's a legitimate career that has remained pretty secluded, and highly coveted. The industry as a whole has flown below the radar of most people. Yet with recent advances in technology, particularly the recent explosion of LinkedIn, this industry's best-kept secrets are just now coming to light. The time has come for the curtain to be pulled back. To invite more women to learn about this elite profession, introduce them to some of the ladies making a great income from home, and offer a step-by-step guide on how to become part of this booming $130 billion machine.

What career choice can offer women the life-work balance that they seek? Please allow this book to properly introduce you to the wonderful world of headhunting. "Why be a desperate housewife when you can be a headhunting housewife?"

While many moms are cooking, cleaning, and searching for a better path, "Headhunting Housewives" will aspire to spend their time hunting, hiring, and happily earning enough money to hire their own nanny and housekeeper so they too can live the life that they deserve! Not only will the pages to follow inform more women of an industry that has managed to remain pretty reclusive through the years, but it can also teach you how to become a home-based headhunter in less than ten weeks! And for those readers who are simply curious to learn what headhunting is all about, this book offers great insider information on how jobs in this country are really filled. This book will serve to educate and demystify the headhunting industry, as well as teach the next generation of headhunting entrepreneurs how the job gets done.

Articles are just starting to emerge on how lucrative the headhunting industry really has become. An industry once thought to be worth $50 billion is estimated in 2012 to be worth over $130 billion. With LinkedIn, the premier recruiting tool in the market today, currently trading over twenty-three times earnings, and large Fortune 100 companies buying recruiting software companies for billions of dollars (such as the recent IBM and Oracle purchases of Kenexa and Taleo), experts are recognizing the recruiting industry as the profit center it is. Companies pay top dollar when it comes to talent acquisition, and headhunters are getting rich filling this need.

Below is a list of some recent headlines and quotes on this phenomenon:

> "Everyone knows that traders, bankers, and lawyers are big money earners, but who are these wealthy recruiters?" (eFinancial Careers, July 2008)

> "Some of the Richest People in the City are Headhunters" (eFinancial Careers, July 2008)

"LinkedIn is Disrupting the Corporate Recruiting Market" (Forbes, February 2012)

"... but the real story is the huge jump in revenues from LinkedIn's recruiting services ("Hiring Solutions"). Revenues in this segment grew by 136% to $84.9 million, making the company the fastest growing public provider of corporate recruiting solutions." (Forbes, February 2012)

"America's Most Surprising Six-Figure Jobs" (Forbes, July 2012)

"Social Recruiting Goes Wild" (Forbes, June 2012)

"Oracle Agrees to Buy Taleo for 1.9 Billion" (Forbes, February 2012)

"Human Resources is the only job on the list, where most, not some, are earning six figures" (Forbes, August 2011)

"To give you a sense of how dramatic this is: LinkedIn's recruiting revenues are now greater than Taleo's (which was just acquired by Oracle for $1.9 billion) and within the year could reach the size of Monster.com." (Forbes, February 2012)

"We estimate that the total worldwide recruiting market is over $130 billion in software, services, content, consulting, and staff. The Talent Acquisition Factbook® has all the numbers." (Forbes, February 2012)

"Executive recruiters, or headhunters, have one mission: matching very specific, top-level talent with very specific, top-level job openings. They are the match-makers of the business world and they're masters of their trade." (ForbesWoman, July 2010)

These quotes may be brow rising to those unfamiliar with the recruiting world, but new technologies are simply starting to shed light on an industry that has been understood to be a cash cow by the lucky few who were in the know. The world may just be waking up to how much money the recruiting industry is really worth, but there's another layer to be uncovered: many of these wealthy headhunters are housewives. Although you may have previously pictured large executive search firm corporate types in suits (Korn Ferry, Heidrick & Struggles, or Christian & Timbers) as the ones getting rich, this book will reveal the true profile of many wealthy headhunters—a confident, career-minded family woman who works from her beautiful home office, dressed like a businesswoman from the waist up (for the video conferencing calls), but trading in her high heels for her comfy Uggs and tailored sweats from the waist down. Six figures in your PJs is no longer a pipe dream, but a reality!

Why You? Why Now?

Have you ever asked yourself questions similar to these?

- How can I work from home, and still make a good six-figure income?
- What business could I start from home that would give me the work-life balance I want?
- Is there a business out there that I could learn quickly and start earning money from home, without having to risk a large capital investment?

If you've asked yourself these types of questions, you've picked up the right book. Headhunting has been one of those secretive careers that you really don't learn about in college. "Human Resources" seems to be the title Headhunters and Recruiters fall under, but I can tell you the best headhunters are not doing the 'human resource' type work you may think of. Recruiting becomes one item on their long list of corporate to do's. Recruiting is really a major undertaking unto itself. It's much closer to Sales than Human Resources. You're actually selling people, and need good sales skills to close the deal. Most Human Resource Managers aren't the sales type. In fact, that's why most HR Departments need to go outside their companies to hire entrepreneurial recruiters, like the "headhunting housewives" you'll learn more about in this book.

So, why does this Recruiting role, and act of "Talent Acquisition" fly so low under the radar, especially when any CEO will tell you that "Hiring" is one of the most important factors in a company's success? Good question. And to be honest, I'm not completely sure of the answer. What I do know is that I stumbled into recruiting after a successful sales career, as have many of the successful recruiters that I have met. It's been one of these careers that seem to find you, or an industry that seems to come onto your radar at the right time of your career. For instance, I remember my first call from a recruiter, when I was just out of college. I assumed he was similar to a telemarketer, until he enlightened me. He was calling me to try and steal me from my current company, and offer me a better opportunity elsewhere. Somewhere in the conversation, he mentioned he used to be a salesperson like myself. Many years later he realized he could make his old salary in just a few select placements each year. I'm not sure if I believed him, since I was just out of college, but his comments always stuck with me. Later in my career, when I was offered a recruiting role, out of the blue, and introduced by my CEO to his current recruiter and "sourcer," the opportunity became very real. They were more than eager to offer me much more than my current salary, if I was able to effectively recruit great sales people just as well as I could sell product. Best move of my life!

Why You?

So, again we ask, why would you want to look closer at recruiting? Money is definitely the first that comes to mind, and what originally excited me and other colleagues about the industry. Yet, after learning more, and becoming an insider in the industry, I quickly learned how many women (and men), were able to easily take this job home. That wasn't important to me when I was 25 and wanting to travel across the country, but when I got a few years older, and didn't want to travel while pregnant, recruiting proved a more valuable career move than I realized. So, money, and ability to work from anywhere you can have a phone and a laptop became another great reason. Later, realizing this is an easy industry to launch a successful "start-up" business from home, proved to bring another very satisfying layer to this Recruiting onion. Money, working from, and entrepreneurial dreams could all be satisfied within the Recruiting Model. And best yet, unlike other industries that take a lot of startup capital or extensive training- recruiting doesn't cost much to start, and if you have the right natural sales skills, not much training is really needed...other than learning the process, and having a mentor to teach you the ropes, so you're not trying to re-invent the wheel!

Why Now?

So, you like the sound of the industry, but why do this now? I'll touch a lot more on this in later chapters, but to keep it simple, social media and the new ways of networking today thru Facebook, LinkedIn, Twitter, and others, have all made Recruiting easier than ever. Finding people is easier, and connecting them with your clients is easier than ever. You may hear comments to the contrary, but I can tell you first hand, that there has never been a better time to become a recruiter, or start your own agency. LinkedIn has not taken away the need for recruiters, it has made it easier for the good headhunters to simply make more money quickly and more efficiently.

Not only has LinkedIn set us recruiters up for easy sourcing and data basing, but this economy here at the end of 2013 is finally about to turn around. Life got tougher for recruiters since 2008, and many cleared out. Here with 2014 ringing in, this leaves a market with space for newcomers to come and grow at a great time of growth for our country. Most analysts and economists agree that our recession is finally coming to a close, as housing numbers and hiring numbers are finally starting to improve for the first time in many years. If you've thought about making a change, and ever considered recruiting- now is when you want to learn how to enter this market and learn the tools needed to be successful over the next decade. The next seven to ten year run, from 2014-2023 is looking to be the golden years in the next business cycle, according to many experts I've talked to on the subject. I tend to agree, looking at all the signs, and listening to colleagues in my industry. Invest in yourself now, and set yourself up in a career that will give you the life and work balance you've been searching for. This isn't a job, and it's even more than a career. It's become a lifestyle for the Headhunting Housewives, and it's a club that any professional woman would want to join. If not to be a headhunter, you certainly want to know the good ones, as you advance thru your career.

Why Me?   Introduction to your Mentor

Now that we've established why you should be learning more about the recruiting world and understand that there's never been a better time to jump into recruiting, you would probably like to know more about the person planning to take you on this little journey. Although this book will properly introduce you to the wonderful world of Headhunting, let me start with introducing myself, the "Headhunting Housewife" who started on this same adventure over a decade ago.   To stay on point, I won't waste space here reviewing my credentials. You can check me out on the web, on LinkedIn, and see referrals and recommendations on my work as a recruiter, business owner, as well as being a mentor. Bottom line, I've got over a decade under my belt successfully earning a six figure income hiring hundreds of people for Fortune 100 Companies, as well as start-ups. You can review my client list on my company website and see my resume on line thru LinkedIn. Clients have included GE, IBM, Siemens, Philips, Florida Power, Next Era, Solectria, Hologic, Cardinal Health, MarketBridge, Vaisala Wind, Agilent, and many others. The CEO's of smaller companies I helped hire for, and the recruiters I helped become better recruiters have written recommendations and mostly private emails of gratitude, but here are some testimonials to give you more insight into my experience, and how I hope to best serve you. After learning more of my background of where I've come from and where I've gone, I hope you come to see that if someone like me could do this, you certainly can do this too!

Testimonials from Recruiter Mentees

"Diane offered me this wonderful opportunity to get back into the work force after taking some time off to raise my children. She was an excellent mentor, teaching me the recruiting business. We began with the basics, sourcing. It enabled me to work part-time...during nap times, school times, or after the kids were asleep at night. I was able to make $1,000 - $2,500 per hire, working at my own pace. The more time I put into it, the more money I made.

Recruiting is a wonderful business for the stay-at-home mom. It enables you to work from home and have the flexibility that is needed when you have young children. As they begin to spend more time in school, you can put in more hours, making more money. Also, as you grow and begin to screen candidates, you earn more per hire. Eventually, you are capable of doing it all, sourcing, screening and working with hiring managers, maximizing your income."

Karen C., Malvern, Pa (part-time recruiter/stay-at-home Mom)

"Diane taught me how to source candidates for local companies that were hiring. At the time, I was fighting breast cancer and wasn't able to work the standard 8-5 job. Diane taught me how to find the right people for the job orders, so that I was able to make $1k -$2k a month in-between my hospital visits. Once I'm cancer free and my hair grows back- I plan to recruit full time, now that I understand how the recruiting process works!

Diane is a great teacher, and invests as much time into you as you're willing to put in yourself!"

Tammy W., Baltimore, MD (part-time recruiter/ stay-at-home Mom)

"I've known Diane for over 6 years, and thanks to her recruiting training- I was able to work from home while my baby was young, learning the recruiting business. Diane taught me the entire recruiting biz, focusing on how to find and close job openings in under 3 months.

I've doubled my earnings this past year- going from being a nanny to being a full time corporate recruiter!"

"At times, Diane believed in me more than I did, especially when I was nervous speaking to CEO's for the first time, and I have yet to finish my college degree! But she believed in me, and helped me close multiple deals that were worth more than $10k each."

Melissa B., Pottstown, Pa (part-time turned full-time recruiter)

"Diane is an incredible mentor, she is extremely knowledgeable in the recruiting and sales field. Diane has a talent of understanding the needs of client and candidate, and always provides the very best quality every time!"

Melissa D. (mentee)

"Diane & I worked together on a project in January 2012. She mentored me in taking a client that was contingent and offering them the retained search model. She was instrumental in guiding me through the placement. We filled the search in two months and it was a success. I highly recommend Diane to anyone looking for recruiting advice whether it is contingent, retained or consulting!"

Luke K, Magellan Search Firm (contingent recruiter to retained recruiter)

"I just wanted to give you the good news, I just received the signed agreement and have landed my first client! THANK YOU! I wouldn't have gotten to this stage without

a little push and accountability. I appreciate your assistance and will keep you updated on the progress."

Chad M. (mentee, business owner)

"Diane helped me become a recruiter in less than the 10 weeks she outlined. We had my first contract by week 7, and I was invoicing my first client by week 9!"

Lisa R. (mentee, business owner)

Testimonials from Client CEO's:

Although the above testimonials were from other people like yourself, looking to learn more about recruiting, it's important to know that the person guiding you along this path has been where you may be trying to go. Below are some quotes from a few Clients:

"Diane O'Brien, founder and Managing Director of SalesSource Recruiting, is a person you can trust to become a true partner when you are in need of recruiting and ramping up a Sales team. She has helped me hire top talent since 1999- including sales teams for GE Medical, IBM, Agilent, and Kodak- to name a few. She is my preferred recruiter that I retain for my own Fortune 100 clients, and would recommend her services to other business owners trying to grow a sales team."

Peter G., CEO, Fusion Sales Partners & Renegade Capital

"I used Diane O'Brien as my exclusive recruiter to hire and ramp up three separate sales teams. She had the highest success rate of finding top sales talent quickly, and was a true partner in the hiring process from start to finish."

Robert G., President, UltraSource, Inc.

> *"When Market-Bridge was first entering the market of indirect sales teams in 2006, we needed to be confident we could hire an A player team quickly and efficiently. Without the help of an HR department, I relied heavily on Diane O'Brien's expertise as a recruiting consultant in finding top talent fast. We hit all of our recruiting goals that first year, as well as our sales goals..."*

Paul C., VP of Business Development, Market-Bridge

Now that you've read a few testimonials, allow me to take the next 10 weeks to prove that you can do it too! But first, you probably want to know exactly how much you can make doing this gig from home.

How much can Headhunters Earn?

Yes, six figures from home is quite possible. I've done it, I know many others who have done it, and I can teach you to do it too. Now, you're probably thinking, yes, there's always the few who accomplish this, but what is average?

Like most things, it really depends on how much energy you want to give this and how much you want to make. My goal was typically $10k per month which meant at least one sales rep earning at least $100k annually. Remember, Headhunters typically earn anywhere from 20-33% of the person's first year salary. So, if you only focus on six figure earners, as I did most of my recruiting career, and can place one a month, which is very conservative, you will surpass your goal of $100k.

If you feel more comfortable hiring or placing candidates on a lower level income, then your income will go down. It's very much like real estate. Do you want to sell the $100k condo or the $1M home? The work isn't that different, but it does take a bit more skill the higher you climb the ladder. I started recruiting sales reps and ended recruiting CEO's and Board of Director Positions. The choice is yours. Do you only want to make $30k part-time and place more readily assessable candidates such as administrative positions? Do you want to work part time placing professionals to earn around $60k? Or you can place high performing professionals or executives and earn the six figures that many headhunters are currently doing.

The choice is yours and it will depend upon your time commitment and skill level. Other than that, all you need is a good mentor that can train you well, and your phone and laptop! A few natural sales skills is always a plus too!

How to Use this Book

This is a step by step, 10 week program on how to learn to become a recruiter. We review each week how to help you reach your goals. I've mentored many successful recruiters, and hope this book will serve to be your private mentor until you connect with one live time, when ready. In fact, as you advance thru the next 10 weeks and next 10 chapters, I would invite you to join a LinkedIn group called NAHBR, National Association of Home Based Recruiters, which will help you find a real life mentor, as you take this journey. By the end of ten weeks, and after completing your weekly checklists of what needs to be done to start and grow your business, you'll be on your way as a recruiter, and as a Headhunting

Housewife. I've included the Weekly goals at the end of this section for you to get a birds-eye view of what you'll be learning. Each week we'll dive into the details and have homework to keep you on track! The Weekly goals are attached, and each chapter will end with a week's checklist of what you should be doing to stay on track.

That's the quick review on how best to use this book, and other books on the topic. Best of luck, and enjoy the adventure! Below is a quick snapshot of the next 10 weeks, if you choose to want to become a "Headhunting Housewife," or "Headhunting Husband!"

The Weekly Goals
Weekly Goal Checklist:

Week 1- Live like a Recruiter

- ✓ Read Chapter 1
- ✓ Office Organization
- ✓ Microsoft Outlook set up
- ✓ Scheduled times for client and candidate calls
- ✓ Schedule dedicated time for mentor calls for next 10 weeks
- ✓ Create signature
- ✓ Learn to add header to documents (resumes)
- ✓ Decide target market
- ✓ Get free training from Monster, learn Boolean tips
- ✓ Create list of target companies to call

Week 2- Find Clients & Get Job Order

- ✓ Review Chapter 1, type of Recruiting Contracts
- ✓ Read Chapter 2
- ✓ Develop 'elevator speech' for obtaining contract
- ✓ Start cold calling client companies
- ✓ Do's and Don'ts of Cold Calling
- ✓ Maintain weekly schedule- cold call during scheduled times at least 20 companies to call per week- Make list
- ✓ Maintain notes and Business Development (3hr time slots)
- ✓ Update list of prospective clients in word document or excel

Week 3- Find Candidates

- ✓ Review Job Board tips, Monster, Career Builder
- ✓ Learn how to post on other boards; craigslist, networking sites, etc.
- ✓ Learn how to mass email candidates
- ✓ Learn how to efficiently save resumes/notes for database
- ✓ Maintain weekly schedule of cold calling/emailing for candidates
- ✓ Develop email template for candidate sourcing

Week 4- Marketing Clients & Candidates

- ✓ This is a Numbers Game, Learn how to work the System

✓ Develop stronger system to where you see how the numbers work

✓ How many calls does it take to get a job order? How many calls does it take before finding a strong candidate?

✓ Are you controlling your day, or is your day controlling you- review with mentor.

Week 5- Process & Matchmaking- Candidates to Client (Send- outs)

✓ Recruiting Process- 1st Phone, 2nd Phone, Video Conferences, Face to Face, Final Offer.

✓ Draft sample email to client- forward to mentor

✓ Draft template email for 'Candidate Prep checklist'

✓ Have Scheduled times for candidate prep (20 minute call)

✓ Have Scheduled times for client confirmation (20 minute call)

✓ Draft template for scheduling confirmations

✓ Review process for send out- Phone, Face to Face, Final Interviews

✓ Your Process Timelines

Week 6- Pushing Job Order to close

✓ Read Chapter 6

✓ Maintain Scheduled calls continuing to develop pipeline for future biz

✓ Review Touch points- follow up calls to client and candidate

✓ Preparing file for back up candidates

Week 7- Throw More Balls in Air

✓ Read Chapter 7

✓ Review Chapter 1-6 because you're starting over

✓ As you work to close your first job order, continue cold call list

✓ Email mentor new client cold calls

✓ Do Not Get Discouraged- "It's the 7 Week Itch" It's only been 7 weeks- Typical learning curve takes 6 months when working it full time- persistence, persistence, persistence!!

✓ Maintain schedule making time for cold calling new clients

✓ Have systems in place: schedule, template emails, timelines

Week 8- Recruiting Balance

✓ Read Chapter 8

✓ Be sure your week equally balances your new work and your family!

✓ First month was learning curve- maintain life balance...create your own schedule all inclusive.

✓ Follow gut- As you network thru clients and candidate- learn to trust gut instincts.

✓ Continue recruiting basics while incorporating new insights.

✓ Work on getting new job order

Week 9- Tools of the Trade: Databases, Bookkeeping, Invoicing

✓ Read Chapter 9
✓ Input all current clients into database
✓ Input all strong candidates into database
✓ Review Accounting & Invoicing
✓ Review Technologies

Week 10- Differentiate Yourself, and Congratulations on becoming a Recruiter!

✓ Read Chapter 10
✓ Congratulate yourself- you've completed the course- you know the recruiting basics!
✓ Determine what makes you different as a recruiter from the millions of others out there.
✓ How can you be different from the rest?
✓ What's your specialty?
✓ Have you developed any niche clients? If not, who are you going to focus on the next few weeks after you complete the course?

Chapter 1

Week 1: You, the Recruiter

First question: SHOULD you be a Recruiter?

We've discussed a bit of what this Headhunting world is all about, so let's learn more about you. Do you really want to be a recruiter? Not just any recruiter, but a home-based recruiter? First, allow me to ask some questions you should ask yourself. Then, I can pull back the curtain a bit to the real life of a home-based recruiter, to see if this is really the job for you.

Where are you in life right now? If you're a busy Mom, with little ones running around, and don't want to hire help with the kids, this probably won't be the job for you, at least not right now. If you're the main 'bread-winner' with the great health benefits needed for your family, and you are responsible for bringing in the consistent income, this may not be the job for you either-at least not to jump into full time. I believe in taking big risks in life when you're following your heart, but always calculated risks, so you don't fall too hard, if you do fall. This is a job you can start to learn part time, in the evenings, and on weekends. In fact, if your desire is simply to "source" and find the candidates, leaving much of the other interviewing to someone else, you can easily do this part time, and learn the business before committing to it further. I've taught many women...and some men... over the years how to become successful home-based recruiters, and they all found their unique path in making it work!

Meet Melissa: A Success Story

My favorite success story is probably Melissa, the nanny I hired for my daughters when they were small. She was my full time nanny for almost 5 years, and my favorite one, as I had a couple before, and a couple after. But she was special- very driven, very honest, and someone I really trusted. When the time came, when the girls were old enough not to need full time nanny-care, I started to teach Melissa about the business she had been watching me do over the years she worked in my home. Although her main dream was to be a stay at home Mom one day, life doesn't always give us what we want. At least not in the beginning, as I suppose life gives us more of what we need, rather than what we want. In Melissa's case, she had her first baby, and realized she needed to make more money. I remember teaching her the ropes, and actually hiring another nanny to watch my kids, and sometimes her baby too, so that I could teach her something that would give her a good life.

Melissa never finished college, and although I recommend this more for women that have the college education, she was tenacious, driven, ambitious, smart, and very charismatic...all the great qualities of a good headhunter. I know there are many non-college educated women that can fit this bill as well; it has just been my experience that the most successful recruiters I've worked with over the years did hold a college degree, so I'm only speaking to what I have found. As anything, there are always exceptions to the rule. In fact, Melissa was one of them. She did great, and was able to support herself fulltime after 6 months.

I hired her for my own company in the beginning, at SalesSource Inc, but considering I was at a place in my career where I wanted to take the summers off and not bring on too many job orders, eventually I had to help push Melissa from the nest. She found another recruiting job very quickly. It was so fun giving her the reference, and knowing I had helped change someone's life. She was, and still is, a successful recruiter. She's made changes over the years to accommodate her growing family as well, but continues in a career that gives her the flexibility that I believe she always desired.

I'm sure this is still a means to an end for her, as it was for me...the main goal is complete freedom with passive income, but how lucky was I, and now for her to have a sustainable job that she loves with opportunities to grow that are boundless. I give this one example, just so you know that this is possible. This was a good example of someone with no college degree, very little business experience that within 6 months became a full time recruiter. But, in this same example you must realize, that she was also not typical. She may have not had her college degree yet, but she had the other important characteristics that were needed in this type job to be successful.

Do you have similar strengths?

Do you have these characteristics? Are you tenacious, do you not give up until you get what you want? Do you enjoy speaking to people, and does your energy seem to actually increase, as you connect with others, even strangers? Are you a positive person?

I think negativity can be felt thru the phone, just like a smile can be felt as well. So, although I'm sure there are many negative type people that have made a lot of money recruiting (in fact, I've met many), I do not believe this is a long-term sustainable role for them. You want your job to fit naturally with who you are. Trying to force it, will just lead to unhappiness, so really be honest in asking yourself these questions, before embarking on this adventure.

So, to move forward on this question of "should" you be a recruiter....there are some other things to ask yourself to make sure this is a viable career path. If you have the personality and aptitude for this role, do you have the space in your life for this? Not just mentally, like when discussing where you are in life, but physically speaking. Do you have a quiet office space to work from? Can you create one, free from distractions, before you ever make your first phone call? I have many things to discuss on this topic that can help lead you to the most effective work space, but to start- just focus on a well-equipped office with working computer, printer, internet, filing,etc.. And above all, a space that is quiet where you can lock yourself away for at least 3 hours at a time, ideally twice a day.

Time & Energy Management

Alright, we have the 'who', the 'where', now onto the 'when.' Like I just mentioned, time management will be key, but so is energy management. When are you at your best, energy wise? Are you a morning person? Or are you more of an afternoon person? I always did the standard 8-5 day for most of my career, however, looking back, I can tell you my best work was done from about 9-

12pm. And then from 1-3. Something about the way the afternoon sun would come thru my office window after 3pm made me want to slow down and enjoy the day, separate from the work. I didn't always have the luxury of stopping at that time, but I learned to have the most important calls, and the 'hard work' of my day, scheduled for those peak hours. Usually trying to do the things I liked the least early in the morning, to get them out of the way.

To this day, separate from work stuff, I do my household duties early as possible. For many years, I had full time help, so basically outsourced the cleaning and laundry to someone else (thank you Recruiting Industry!) But these days, although I still have someone come in to clean, I prefer not to have someone lingering in the house during the day, since it's just my husband and I, while the kids are in school. Yet, the daily chores, that are not so fun, still need to get done. Therefore, I still follow this rule, and make sure one load of laundry is complete before my daughters head out the door at 6:50am. The kitchen is clean from breakfast, and the house is completely tidy before I step out to walk the dog by 7:30ish...at least when the weather is nice!

I suppose I may be giving too much detail here, but I'm simply giving these real life examples, so you know how important this time and energy management is to your success. It's the only way you'll manage to create a life balance that you will love, while being able to also enjoy your career. For me, I'm not as effective in my office, unless the more important world, of my home, which is outside my office doors, is clean and peaceful. And then when able to turn my attention to my work, I would first accomplish the task that I wanted to get out of the way. For me, this was the sourcing of candidates, which is the "research" part of the job. This is the part I outsourced very often, but when I had to do it myself, as you will in learning this job, you will need to give hours to researching candidates, hunting the job boards and scanning resumes.

By having a dedicated time, those first 2-3 hours in the morning, I would get it done, and then have the fun part of the job for me left ahead. For me, that has always been talking to people on the phone, offering something that I think would make their life better (in this case, it was an opportunity for a better job). This part of recruiting always re-energized me, and kept me on a high note until I ended my work day around 4-5. I always used 8-9am as organizational time, as well as the 4-5pm time frame, and that worked well for me too. So, whatever time frames work for you, is what you need to figure out. Obviously, it will need to fit in with the best times for your candidates and clients too, but there's plenty of room in a work day and evening to carve out where you want to spend your time.

A friend of mine, a bit opposite of me, loved to research and read thru resumes, so she would take a few hours in her favorite part of the day to go to a Starbucks with her coffee, and sit for 2-3 hours simply reviewing resumes and making notes of who she wanted to speak to later on. So, whatever works for you is what you need to figure out. Continue to think about the time that would work best for you, and then build your office day around that. Think of the ideal work day, plan it, and then live that plan. It sounds easy, but you'll see how fast the world will want to take over your peaceful day. It takes a lot of discipline, courage, ability to say no, while also being flexible, and an overall ability to never lose the big picture, as you enter each new work day.

Ideally, you want to be the one running your life, not your life running you. So start out with that end in mind, and go from there! Hopefully, this has given you some insight into becoming a headhunting housewife, and if it is a career that would work well for you!

WHY do you *really* want to be a recruiter?

We discussed the SHOULD you become a recruiter, but before we dive into this plan of HOW, let's make sure we understand your WHY you really want to be a recruiter. We should really start with why do you want to be an entrepreneur? Because if you realize at some point in this book that recruiting is not for you, all your time so far has not been in vein. Chances are you've been looking for an idea to inspire you enough to start your own business, and just because recruiting may start to look like it's not the right fit for you, that doesn't mean that you are not meant to still search to find the right spot.

I can name countless times where I started down one path to only end up in a completely different place than I first intended to go. However, I do believe those first steps were still meant to be, because if I wouldn't have taken the first steps, and made certain contacts, I would have never been led to the 'better' place I ended up.

For example, I once went to consult for a new company to help them recruit, and ended up traveling to amazing locations and became more of a business developer than recruiter. Or the time I reached out to a company to try out some new recruiting technology, and after speaking to them at length, and getting to know them, they later asked me to represent their company on a news program, as their spokesperson. Or, what about the big stuff, like when you go someplace to have fun with girlfriends, and stumble upon your now husband. So, in business, just like life, remember that each path has its purpose, and one perceived failure can turn into a larger success.

I can count numerous examples from my experience in hiring, as well as watching employees that were let go, how one job's failure does not necessarily reflect on that person's value. I can tell you with confidence that a "failure" or "C- Player" at one company and position, can be a "success story" and an "A player" at another company with a different culture. If you are having success with a new venture, continue on. If you seem to hit a wall, find out where life takes you when you look at other pathways.

You can use whatever you learn here to take with you and start a successful recruiting company that will help you reach all of your dreams. Or, take this information, and apply it to any area that you would to start something new. The 10 mini-chapters in the "Happy Headhunter" eBook are designed to create the habits that help new entrepreneurs get into shape, mentally, physically, spiritually for a new venture. If you get stuck on a chapter, and it hits you that this isn't what you really want, then read those tips to start setting yourself up to think more like an entrepreneur. The actual area of your expertise will show up when you're ready!

So, having said all of that, here's the big question for today. What is your WHY for doing this? Really take time to think about this, because before we dive into the technicalities of what a Headhunting Housewife does, you'll need to write up a business plan. And I'm talking a simple business plan. Figuring out the why, the what, the when, the how much, and so on. At each section, you need to ask yourself the right questions. So, start with the why, and take your time. Pray on these questions, write them down, meditate on them, and sleep on them. Have a little time each day to remember the big reasons you are doing all of this. Because you will get lost in the minutia of it all, and there will be days where you will want to just forget the whole thing. It's going to feel like a waste of time. You're not alone. We all go thru these emotions. Whether you're starting a business, trying to lose weight, trying to eat healthier, trying to improve a relationship- you name it. Think of examples in your life, and what it took to keep you going.

Have those answers ready on your business plan, so you can refer to it when you want to give up. I've never really made a dream board before, yet I'm already having my daughters learn to do this. I can say I've always written my dreams down, and they typically do come true. Not at the time I want, but eventually, it comes around. And again, when they haven't seemed to appear at all, later as time goes by, I can see that I ended up someplace better in the long run. So, your business plan and your dreams will change as you do. But start with a simple plan. Figure out what will keep you going. Are you doing this for your family, your husband, wife, children? Do you need the money to help fuel a college fund, or 2nd home that you've always dreamt of? Do you want to set an example for your kids that all things are possible when you can align your unique gifts in a way that serves the world?

And I know we should all just wish for joy, peace, happiness, and health. But I see nothing wrong with also wanting nice homes, amazing travel adventures, fun cars, or just happy money to spend on what you want, when you want. Desiring money is not a bad thing, as long as you understand the motivation behind it. How will money serve you and the world? Think of how the money you wish for can not only serve you and your family, but think about the real good your hard work can do by serving your community and world?

The more you can align your successes with making the world a better place, the more abundance seems to flow to you. We've all heard these things before, but it doesn't hurt to reiterate these secrets of success over and over, so we can remember them and use them!

Find mentors to remind you of this. Utilize YouTube for instant mentor gratification. Now, more than ever in our history, thanks to technology, with a few clicks of the button, you have a world of support out there. Whether thru books like this, mentors on the other end of a phone, or watching a video clip of someone who can inspire you to be better... now is the best time to become who you want to be!

Go for it, don't be afraid, figure out why you want this, and make it happen. One hour at a time, one day at a time, season by season.

How to Start Living like a Recruiter

Let's get back to talking about how exactly you are going to now become a recruiter! Whether you are reading about recruiting for the first time, and still deciding if this is the career path for you, or if you are ready to jump right in and begin. This book is designed to teach you not only about the world of recruiting, but how to start living like a recruiter, and how to become a home based recruiter over the next 10 weeks.

Like anything in life, it's all about forming good habits, and establishing best practices within your day to get the results you desire. If you want to become a "Headhunting Housewife," you need to start acting like one. This includes learning successful habits, as well as implementing time management skills needed to get the job done, and also learning the overall methods of placing people in new jobs. Although home based recruiting is a very lucrative career choice that can give you a work-life balance that few people get to enjoy, this is not an easy career.

Recruiting is highly competitive, and although you can learn the skills to become a six-figure home based recruiter, not all of you reading this will be able to make that happen. The good news is that perhaps you shoot high, and come in somewhere a little lower, but still end up with a very rewarding paycheck and career. The bad news is that some of you may try to become successful in this new role, when perhaps the characteristic traits that are needed (tenacity, determination, sales skills, time management, charisma, discipline) do not come naturally, and this becomes an unsuccessful venture. My goal for you is to help you determine if this is the right career path for you before spending $1 or any more than a couple hours of your time as you research the mysterious world of home based recruiting.

Become a Headhunter in 10 Weeks!

To learn from someone who has done it herself, can prove to be invaluable. It not only saves time and money for the housewives out there that may not be the exact fit, but also serves to help the housewives out there that have the right skill sets. This book aims to make more women aware of this amazing career path, and help future headhunters learn the ropes to become successful within 10 weeks.

You have seen the outline of how the next 10 weeks and 10 chapters should progress. You are going to have ups and downs, highs and lows, like anything in life. If it's not meant to be, you may drop off within a few weeks, and move onto to other things in life that will be a more suitable path. If this is meant to be something that you should learn about, I hope to be just the person you were looking for to teach you the ins and outs of being a successful home based recruiter! Good luck, and be sure to not only look forward to the money that will end this journey, but also to enjoy the ride of learning something new and exciting, and for having the guts to become your own boss and join the ranks of many, happy, and successful Headhunting Housewives (and some brave Headhunting Husbands!)

Setting Up your Office

Have an organized office. You'll need your clean, quiet work space, with a large desk to write on, your laptop, your phone with a headset preferably, lots of paper and printer. You'll want your calendar ready to go that you can schedule appointments in. With the IPhone now a days, the calendar and schedules are so much easier, but otherwise, keep your calendar on outlook since its easy access with your emails, and syncs well.

You'll need your signature set up, with your company name and logo if needed. You should learn how to add headers and footers thru word documents so you can add them to resumes that you submit. It's always a good idea to have your information on the resumes, so the client interviewing the candidate will also remember where they got the good talent from. Start learning Monster, CareerBuilder, Indeed, LinkedIn. Join Facebook if you are not on because they will progress similar to LinkedIn to where you can use it as part of your personal database and contact information. LinkedIn is the best one for that now, but Monster and CareerBuilder are still old standbys that most recruiting companies still subscribe to, although they would never admit that to clients! I can tell you that in the early years, over half my finds came from Monster. The other half were usually referrals from people I contacted thru someone on Monster of another job board. In more recent years, LinkedIn became my strongest source, other than my personal database, but you want to get familiar with all the technologies and stay current. Bullhorn is another my current company utilizes and loves. I'm not doing the actual recruiting as much these days, but I became familiar with Bullhorn, and do think it's a great tool. Especially since it integrates so well with LinkedIn.

Keep in mind, all of these databases and job boards offer free training, so take advantage of these free conference calls and webinars. They will ramp you up quickly, and this should be part of your schedule this week to really start learning the ins and outs of recruiting.

Finding a Mentor to help you on a weekly basis over the next 10 weeks is also critical. I've done this for many friends, students, recruiters, housewives turned into headhunting housewives, but if I'm not available, I can recommend ways for you to find mentors. YouTube is great for this. Lots of people put lots of great free information out there now a days, so please take full advantage. I have also posted a few training clips so far, but plan on doing more webinars and the like to get you information that will be very helpful. Having said all this, there's nothing than having a real live person on the other end of the phone. Even if you hire a consultant an hour a week, or a 30 minute call to make sure you are on track, this can be the difference.

There's a service I recently found helpful called liveperson.com. You can view pictures and backgrounds of people in your field of interest, and you can speak for free the first time. You can then agree to a fee that will serve both of you well for whatever you're looking for. I would recommend cross checking the person you like with LinkedIn or Facebook to make sure you get a broad sense of exactly what their expertise is, and to make sure they are legitimate. And usually a free first phone call can give you a good sense whether they are the one to help you over the next 10 weeks.

This first week is also a good time to start developing a list of target markets and target companies that you want to call into to try and get business from. I'll cover this at length, and separate from reading this in a book, speaking to someone live who has done this already can help save you a lot of time. Remember to not try and re-invent the wheel. Whatever area you get stuck at, there are plenty of people out there wanting to help you get unstuck, so get creative. Search the internet, search YouTube, search the bookstore, search LivePerson, or other mentor sites, and find whatever resources you need to make the next 10 weeks happen.

Setting Up your Filing System

I worked with online and hard copies when starting out. Hard copies will be for you to take notes, especially when interviewing a Client for the first time to understand their needs. It's useful for scribbling notes on the resumes during your interview with candidates. It's also best to input the notes into the database system right afterwards, or else you'll always be paper bound. If you can type quick while talking, and can go paperless from the beginning, that's ideal. I wasn't able to go truly paperless until I no longer had the interviews with the candidates. Even today with clients, I still take hand held notes, and later put them into my database.

Setting up your Database

I mentioned the various software out there, and I've tried many of them. Remember, databases are only as good as what you put into them. I like keeping things simple, and even though I had my computer scientist Father (thanks Dad!), help with my own custom version within Outlook....good old Outlook will work fine. I found it to be the easiest since it's on the same page as your email. Most of the software integrates with your email, or links you to it, but you just need the basics, capturing numbers, emails, area and zip codes, and notes. If you plan on growing to have many employees, you'll have to figure out something more, but even when I had a few recruiters working with me, Outlook worked well.

Again, LinkedIn has changed the World of Recruiting regarding keeping track of your contacts, but you'll still want a place to keep more detailed notes and information, as well as wanting to use

"Email Blitz Campaigns" later....we'll speak more on that down the line. For now, you just want to have a system to keep files on all of the important contact you make in a given day. Each person should be quickly notated and if you only get an email and cell phone number early on, you're setting yourself up for success in the future. This was an area my impatience got the best of me, and for the first few years, I lost a lot of valuable contacts since I did not take the time to store their information as I did my work. Don't think you'll do it at the end of the day or tomorrow, because most of you won't. You need to do it while you move thru your day and make a daily habit of building your own database of clients and candidates as you work.

Setting Up Computer & Phone

You'll need a few things set up on your computer to you the most efficient and organized recruiters. Here's a quick checklist to get started this week:

- Microsoft Business- You'll need Microsoft Word and Outlook.
- Set up a professional email address you will use for recruiting
- Save Signatures for emails.
- Learn to put headers and footers on paperwork

Phone

Get a headset from Staples or somewhere this week. You'll enjoy speaking on the phone more with it, and now a days you won't hang yourself with the wire like I did for over 7 years! Although many people have gotten rid of their landlines, and use only their cell to save money, you definitely want a dedicated business phone in your home. Clear communication is the most important part of your job. You're doing interviews all day by phone, and you do not want a bad connection for these calls. You can also set up your phones to automatically forward calls to your cell phone when traveling. Caller ID is a must as well, so you know who is calling you. Don't be so quick to just answer the phone every time it rings. Especially when you get very busy putting lots of calls out to potential candidates. Be selective in how you spend your phone time. And if you've dedicated a few hours to research time, only answer the phone if it's from a strong candidate you've been waiting to talk to. The others can leave messages, and allows you to control your day a bit more. I would however answer the phone every time a potential client calls you, when possible!

Setting Up your Schedule

Your Daily Calendar- Set it each morning, so you're in control of your day. I'm going to make it as simple as possible to start:

9am-12: Cold calls to companies for job orders

1-3pm: Search for candidates to fill job orders

Obviously, this is a very basic example, but the point is to simply have an agenda each day. Things will get more fluid the busier you become, but you want to stay in control of your day whether you have one job order you're working or ten job orders...start the good habits, and outline your schedule from day one! As you learn your own habits, and when you work the smartest, take notes on this, and build a schedule around it. If you can improve your process by learning when you are at your best, and work to those time slots, the more efficient you'll be, and you'll run your schedule and calendar like a pro. Nothing feels better then setting up your schedule for the day, and being able to check off all the boxes, knowing you control your schedule, and it no longer controls you!

Recruiting 101

Understanding Recruiting Terminology

Let's Review some Recruiting 101 Basics regarding contracts, job orders, job descriptions and more so you know more of the lingo in this business.

Job Orders: The job order is an internal form where you have a template of all the right questions to ask the client. It's the "who" they are looking for, "where" do they need the person, "what" qualifications and experience are they looking for, "how" long before they need to hire this person, etc. Many companies don't always have a formal job request or job order- but either way, you'll want to use your own Job Order Form (see attached that we use at SalesSource) to be sure and capture all the needed details that you'll want to gather from your client on that first phone call. It is from this information that you can build your job description.

Job Description: The job description will be used more on the candidate side, as this is the description of the job, and provide all the details you'll want to give to your candidates. We'll cover this in detail in Chapter 3 on the Candidate questions. Keep in mind the Job Order is almost more of an internal document that you fill out during your first call to the client. Your job description will be developed off of your job order, but can be shared with candidates online.

Contracts: You typically do not want to work a job order unless you have a formal contract in place with your customer. I have made the mistake of working a job for a new client without the formal contract in place. Especially in situations where I personally knew the customer, and got to work on the job before signing a contract. You don't typically want to do this. Always try to get the contract signed before you make one phone call. This sounds obvious, but you may find yourself in the situation where you trust your client, and signing on a dotted line seems like a forgotten formality. However, communication can often be perceived differently, so you really want to try to put something in writing first, before working the deal.

Understanding Types of Recruiting Contracts

Recruiters usually work one of three ways...Contingent, Exclusive, or Retained. And later, similar to what I did, make some creative deals in-between. I personally started as a Contingent recruiter, worked my way up to Exclusive Contracts, which basically came with the confidence after performing very well for a long term contingent client. After a few years, I then graduated to Retained. Contingent means that you may have the job order, along with 2 or 5 other agencies. It's a free for all, extremely competitive, and often tougher to close the job. You're not only competing with other recruiters to find the right candidate the fastest, but you are also competing for the Hiring Managers time. Their schedule is now being filled with interviews from you and other agencies.

Once you gain confidence in yourself as a recruiter, and gain your client's confidence, it shouldn't be a far jump to show your client why using you exclusively is actually to their benefit. We'll discuss this more further.

Exclusive Contracts means the client has agreed to only use you for the search, and you exclusively. You still do not get paid until they hire your candidate, but at least you have more control of the search, and the schedule since you're dealing one on one with the Hiring Manager.

Retained Contracts had always been the goal for me. Now I do have recruiter friends that prefer contingent or exclusive because they don't like the pressure of being the only recruiter on the job, but I've never been of this thinking. In fact, I created something in-between exclusive and retained for many of my clients.

Fees

On a retained search, you typically get paid a percentage to simply start the search. Perhaps 1/3 to start search, 1/3 half way thru, and 1/3 on candidates start date. At times, I would often not ask for the full retainer up front, but would get a smaller amount in the form of an "engagement fee," and later work towards more money up front.

This way, if they decided to hire internally instead, or change the territory 2 weeks into the search, I would still get paid for my time. I'll discuss more of these details later, along with how to convince your client to move to this exclusive or retained level.

Okay, so we have a quick review on the job order and the contracts, but how do you get either of these to start? Phone time, research time, phone time, phone time, phone time! Let's ask some basic business plan questions, and then start on the path to finding and landing your first client!

Develop a One day Business Plan

I found this YouTube site from Tori Johnson after I wrote this chapter, but it fits what we just spoke about very well. Check out Tori, and her cause in empowering women at womenforhire.com.

The best advice I can give to doing a business plan, especially for us busy women or mothers, is to keep it simple. If the job of creating a business plan becomes too daunting or overwhelming, you might not do one at all. Which to be honest, was me, with my first business. But if you keep it simple, and just cover the basic questions...why, what, who, when, where, how much you'll be further ahead than most!

The Weekly Goals
10 Weeks to Success

Below is the list of Goals you should review each week to stay on target with becoming a recruiter over the next 10 weeks. It can often take longer than this to finalize your first deal, as the recruiting process takes 8-12 weeks typically in my experience, yet if you follow the same time-line as the typical recruitment process, you have the best chance of setting yourself up for recruiting success. Remember, it usually takes 2weeks to source, 2 weeks to schedule, 2 weeks to interview, 2 weeks for candidates to give notice, and often a week or 2 voided out from human error (schedule changes or missed phone calls, etc.) So these 10 weeks are running on a typical schedule, and are used as a guideline. You'll fine tune this to fit your own schedule later, but I hope this serves you well as a baseline until you are established on your own! Good luck!

<u>10 Week Sessions Available;</u>

Fall Session: Sept-Nov,
Winter Session: Jan-March,
Spring Session: April- June
Summer Session- Closed: "At the Beach!"

Weekly Goal Checklist:

Week 1- Live like Recruiter

- ✓ Read Chapter 1
- ✓ Office Organization
- ✓ Microsoft Outlook set up
- ✓ Scheduled times for client and candidate calls
- ✓ Schedule dedicated time for mentor calls for next 10 weeks
- ✓ Create signature
- ✓ Learn to add header to documents (resumes)

✓ Decide target market

✓ Get free training from Monster, learn Boolean tips

✓ Create list of target companies to call

Week 2- Find Clients & Get Job Order

✓ Review Chapter 1, type of Recruiting Contracts

✓ Read Chapter 2

✓ Develop 'elevator speech' for obtaining contract

✓ Start cold calling client companies

✓ Do's and Don'ts of Cold Calling

✓ Maintain weekly schedule- cold call during scheduled times (3hr time slots)

✓ Have at least 20 companies to call per week- Make list

✓ Maintain notes on promising clients in word document

Week 3- Find Candidates

✓ Review Job Board tips, Monster, Career Builder

✓ Learn how to post on other boards; craigslist, networking sites, etc.

✓ Learn how to mass email candidates

✓ Learn how to efficiently save resumes/notes for database

✓ Maintain weekly schedule of cold calling/emailing for candidates

✓ Develop email template for candidate sourcing

Week 4- Marketing Clients & Candidates

✓ This is a Numbers Game, Learn how to work the System

- ✓ Develop stronger system to where you see how the numbers work
- ✓ How many calls does it take to get a job order?
- ✓ How many calls does it take before finding a strong candidate?
- ✓ Are you controlling your day, or is your day controlling you- review with mentor.

Week 5- Process & Matchmaking- Candidates to Client (Send-outs)

- ✓ Recruiting Process- 1st Phone, 2nd Phone, Video Conference, Face to face Interview, final offer.
- ✓ Draft sample email to client- forward to mentor
- ✓ Draft template email for 'Candidate Prep checklist'
- ✓ Have Scheduled times for candidate prep (20 minute call)
- ✓ Have Scheduled times for client confirmation (20 minute call)
- ✓ Draft template for scheduling confirmations
- ✓ Review process for send out- Phone, Face to Face, Final Interviews
- ✓ Your Process Timelines

Week 6- Pushing Job Order to close

- ✓ Read Chapter 6
- ✓ Maintain Scheduled calls continuing to develop pipeline for future biz
- ✓ Review Touch points- follow up calls to client and candidate
- ✓ Preparing file for back up candidates

Week 7- Throw More Balls in Air

✓ Read Chapter 7

✓ Review Chapter 1-6 because you're starting over

✓ As you work to close your first job order, continue cold call list

✓ Email mentor new client cold calls

✓ Do Not Get Discouraged- "It's the 7 Week Itch" It's only been 7 weeks- Typical learning curve takes 6 months when working it full time- persistence, persistence, persistence!!

✓ Maintain schedule making time for cold calling new clients

✓ Have systems in place: schedule, template emails, timelines

Week 8- Recruiting Balance

✓ Read Chapter 8

✓ Be sure your week equally balances your new work and your family!

✓ First month was learning curve- maintain life balance...create your own schedule all inclusive.

✓ Follow gut- As you network thru clients and candidate- learn to trust gut instincts.

✓ Continue recruiting basics while incorporating new insights.

✓ Work on getting new job order

Week 9- Tools of the Trade: Databases, Book-keeping, Invoicing

✓ Read Chapter 9

✓ Input all current clients into database

✓ Input all strong candidates into database

✓ Review Accounting & Invoice Templates

✓ Review Technologies to use in your business

Week 10- Differentiate Yourself, and Congratulations on becoming Recruiter!!

✓ Read Chapter 10

✓ Congratulate yourself- you've completed the course! You know the recruiting basics.

✓ Determine what makes you different as a recruiter from the millions of others out there.

✓ How can you be different from the rest?

✓ What's your specialty?

✓ Have you developed any niche clients? If not, who are you going to focus on the next few weeks after you graduate the course?

Review Week 1 Goal Checklist

- ✓ Read Chapter 1
- ✓ Office Organization
- ✓ Microsoft Outlook set up
- ✓ Scheduled times for client and candidate calls
- ✓ Schedule dedicated time for mentor calls for next 10 weeks
- ✓ Create signature
- ✓ Learn to add header to documents (resumes)
- ✓ Decide target market
- ✓ Get free training from monster, learn Boolean tips
- ✓ Find Mentor- Search youtube.com, liverperson.com, etc.
- ✓ Develop account on LinkedIn, Facebook, others
- ✓ Create list of target companies to call
- ✓ Create Simple Business Plan- One pager.

Links to visit and review this week:

Visit NAHBR.com

Visit Monster

Visit LinkedIn

Visit CareerBuilder

Visit Indeed.com

Visit Hoovers.com

Diane O'Brien

Chapter 2

Week 2: Clients & Job Orders

Clients

Finding Clients is definitely a very important and necessary part of this new endeavor! As before, we'll start with asking the right questions, and working our way backwards. You'll notice similarities when focusing on Clients and Candidates, and you'll develop a similar process on both sides. You will be asking yourself the same set of questions as we would ask ourselves on the candidate side. Think of where, what, who, how and when?

We will also start with a general knowledge of where you are going to start seeking client companies, and then drill down to the specifics of exactly where and how you get a client.

"Where" to find Clients (In General)? What is your niche market?

The main question is where are you going to find clients? This leads us to the question of what market place do you want to play in? Where are you going to find your clients? Think about where your interests have been. For example, if you were a nurse in a previous life, why not try recruiting nurses for hospitals. If you came from a sales background, like I did, why not transition into hiring sales people in the same industry you came from? Unless you left a marketplace or industry that you felt was uninspiring or a dead end, it usually makes the most sense to play this game where you already have some experience. It's just simpler.

Having said this, after over a decade recruiting in the Medical Industry, I made a strategic jump into the Clean Tech Industry. I'll speak more on that later, as after a solid 10+ year run in medical, I wanted the next 10 years to be in the next exciting and booming industry- and Clean Tech was, and still is it! I'll have a lot of advice for you if you want to break into this industry, but for now, I'll keep this segment simple.

Whatever marketplace you choose, the rest of the recruiting basics will stay the same. The process doesn't really change if you're hiring a salesperson to sell medical equipment, or a sales person to sell solar panels. Even between the positions, the process is relatively the same. You may have to add some time on the calendar when hiring for higher level executive positions like a VP of Sales, or a CEO, but the process of how to find and get the person hired is pretty much the same.

What was my Niche Market?

For most recruiters, including myself, the most natural progression is to recruit in the industry you're currently working. I'll use this opportunity to give you my personal story of figuring out which markets I wanted to play in, and how that evolved over the past decade or so.

It's important to see that where you start, may not always be where you end up, but you have to start somewhere, and keeping it simple usually works best.

As I've mentioned in my introduction, I was a medical sales rep, so I began my recruiting career hiring for medical sales companies. I originally started with sales reps only, which went for about $10-$15k a placement. I continued to specialize in this market, and slowly added managers for $20-$25k a placement, and Director level positions for around $30- $36k. I stayed at this level for the bulk of my recruiting years, while "working a desk". These are the fee structures I've worked in for the past decade, but every industry and level is different. If you're hiring administrative help, the fees may only be $6k, but if you're hiring CEO's they can be $100k. I'll never forget how shocked I was when the CEO of a company I hired sales reps for $10k a pop told me he had hired a firm that he retained for $100k to find him his next COO. They never found him his guy- but they were paid the $100k all the same.

I had wished I was at that level, looking back. The company was a very large and reputable retained executive firm. I didn't realize how big they were, but I remember meeting them in their large boardroom discussing the position that my company needed help filling. The two men, my CEO, and the other recruiter's CEO, stayed to talk contracts, and I had the unique experience of having this large retained executive search firm's curtain being pulled back. The recruiter took me back to her desk, and showed me how they went about finding people. I remember being surprised that except for the larger office with better city views (keep in mind even then, as a Human Resources Recruiter, I still negotiated to work mainly from home), I realized she wasn't doing anything different than I was doing. The process was similar, the database and search methods were the same. Yet, at that time, only being in my twenties, hiring C-Level people on a retainer seemed out of my league. It wasn't even on my radar. Funny, looking back, that not only have I been able to play in that game for the past several years, but I'm about ready to move onto other fun things that I never thought I'd be privileged enough to do! Goes to show that you should never say never, and always dream big!

I think it's good for you to know the sky is the limit in this industry. When my goal was only sales rep jobs, since that was my comfort zone, I became rather content in that world, doing most jobs for a $10-$30k commission range. It wasn't till many years later, I gained the confidence to move into higher fees and better contracts. I could have gone after those day 1, I just didn't know enough yet.

As I mentioned earlier, for me deciding to make that jump ended up with me deciding to jump into a new industry also. Until that point, I was exclusive and retained, but at lower numbers. It wasn't till I was able to get behind the scenes again of another retained executive search firm, almost 8 years later, that new worlds opened up to me, once again.

Not only did I want to 'up my game,' but I also wanted to do some other things at this point in my life and career. I wanted more travel again to warm, beautiful locations. I wanted to meet different people, at different levels of the game, outside the medical sales and healthcare industry that I had grown accustomed to. This later proved to be an exciting new adventure leading me to understand more of how small start-ups actually start up. I learned who actually hires that first CEO, and met the people doing it. I was introduced to the Private Equity world, and met the Venture Capitalists that were investing a lot of money into Clean-Technology companies. They were needing to hire talented leaders to make it all happen, so recruiting was once again a nice entry point into a new world to explore. Recruiting and Biz Dev became new again as I visited Silicon Valley and Sand Hill Road in Palo Alto. Travels to LA, Palm Springs, and San Francisco on a conference circuit was something that went past my original goals of simply looking to hire at higher levels retained. In fact, now that I look back, when things become more 20/20 and clear, my purpose for moving into Clean Tech was not only to keep life interesting, but also opened my eyes to things that took my focus more and more off the numbers. I was happily traveling to these locations in the winter, and was gaining the new experiences I was craving, while learning new aspects of Recruiting. It was fun again, and helped me remember that the fun experiences trump the commissions every time. I still always made sure to add more value to the companies I consulted for, than whatever I cost them. It was a strange year in my life in 2008, making less money than I'd made in my old market, yet feeling happy to be out in the world more, being exposed to new industries and new types of people.

Although the contracts finally came, as did other job offers for my consulting services (thanks to LinkedIn, where CEO's would find me, and call me for Consulting gigs!), something shifted for me by this point. I wasn't sure if I was just comfortable enough to not have to work as hard anymore, or if perhaps the hunger and desire that I started my career with, was leaving me? The excitement I use to feel with a big commission check was not as important as the excitement I received from my travels and the experiences I was having. There were times where I worked long hours, and didn't close a specific big commission deal, yet I had a feeling I was right where I was supposed to be, for that time, and that I was now searching for something more significant than only money from my business endeavors.

This is again, where I was deciding to change course, and play in a different sandbox for this part of my life. This is when I began to want to help others more, and teach other moms or young recruiters, how to take the ride I had just taken. That was my original intent with starting a site called NAHBR, the National Association of Home Based Recruiters. I had trained plenty of recruiters over the years to help make my business more profitable, but thought it would be good to create a platform to help other home based recruiters connect. I was mentoring other recruiters, or just helping give advice. However, I'm sad to admit that as soon as large contracts or opportunities came up, I let the mentoring slide, and didn't put the free seminars and classes, or this book together, back then as I had hoped.

The good news is that after more productive runs that fueled me to have free time, I'm turning down jobs to take that time and get this book complete. To start up NAHBR again, and have it be a place for other home based recruiters or headhunting housewives, to reach out and connect to one another. This time, since I'm nearing 40 years old, I'm more motivated than ever, to make this about giving back, as I grow into a new exciting future for myself. Life has never let me down before, so I decided to give more hours of my day, and more of my money, to help start something that will ideally benefit many others, especially focusing on women empowerment. I figured only good stuff could come from that! So, that's my 'why,' and part of my motivation. I know "win-win" is grossly overused, but so far in my mentoring, the students feel that I've given them more than the time had cost them, and yet, I always feel that I enjoyed the experience more than the money that came with it! Guess that's a true win-win!

Where to Find Clients (Specifically)?
Job Boards

There are several ways to find that first company to target as a client. The best way is if you already have an in. Did you work for the company before- which was my case in landing my first client. Do you already know a company that is hiring thru the grapevine? Go onto the free job boards- Monster, CareerBuilder, Indeed, and the countless smaller ones to see who is posting jobs. You will see what companies are already hiring, and you need to find that person who is interviewing for the company. You'll find their contact info thru the web, and tracking down their contact info from company websites. It sounds confusing, but trust me, this is easy compared to the "old days" when you couldn't Google most people, or have cell phone numbers that stay the same. There are lots of details you'll have to learn, but basically- go for the cell, office numbers, and email addresses. Try starting with emails to make the live call a bit warmer. There are lots of companies out there and most of them need help hiring. And remember, you only need one company to hire you. A growing company can make you a lot of money if you become their preferred, and later exclusive or retained recruiter, so you can, and will find the company that's a right fit for you. From there- you visit the website to find out information on that particular company.

You can access free online information sites like hoovers.com or zoom info, to learn more about other competitive companies in that space. Once you land your first job order, you will most likely find the path of least resistance is to get other job orders in that same niche.

Networking for Jobs

Networking within your industry is the key. You will find that when you start making calls to companies searching an opening, it's like you've started on a pathway that seems to take on a trail of its own. Your job is to follow that path, a bit like a Private Investigator would go from one lead to the next. This method will repeat itself when you start to look for candidates, as I mentioned earlier. One client call will lead you to another client, and one candidate call often leads you to other candidates. Sometimes, a candidate call ends up giving you another job order. Those are the best.

If I tend to repeat myself a bit thru this process, keep in mind a person often needs to hear something multiple times for it to sink in, so like in life, I'd rather over communicate certain truths to you versus missing something, so please bear with me...hopefully the repetition, although sometimes annoying, will be beneficial!

Who are your clients? Who is your audience?

If you want to play in sales industry, your clients (the who?) may be sales managers and HR managers. The Market place, or your new sandbox, will answer the 'what' question. The market place could be the Medical market, for example. Where? Where do you find these Hiring Managers and Sales Managers in the Medical Market. Here you will develop your niche further. If in Medical, maybe you feel comfortable in lower end disposable market, or pharmaceuticals. Or, maybe you came from a high end capital sale, and want to help hire sales reps that sell MRI's to hospitals. Remember in choosing your market that your fee will be determined by how much the candidate you place makes in any given year. Based upon that idea, as well as to my own experience and comfort level, I chose six figure sales reps.

How to find clients?

And finally, the How? How do you find clients? Well, you start making contact with the people in the market we just described. Develop a target list of clients and find contact information for each one, and get to work. You will be calling lots of people here, so get comfortable on the phone. I did telemarketing and advertising sales thru college to help pay for my school, so I was use to selling over the phone. You'll need to learn these skill sets, and be able to connect quickly with clients over the phone or later, via email.

That's it, in a nutshell. So, once you have an interested party for a client, you'll utilize the recruiting contracts, take advantage of the recruiting lingo we learned, and move into how to develop the Job Description. And again, your Job Order & Job Description will be developed by asking the right set of questions. If you can remember this, you'll be good to go!

Now, regarding the 'when?' That will be determined by training classes you may be hiring to, or other factors, so we'll answer that later, and learn to develop your own 'when' separate from what the client dictates, so your goals are not contingent on them. You can still stay in control of the 'when,' even when your clients are giving you the deadlines. But this factor will come into play after we cover more on getting the job order and job description.

So, you've decided on the market, and what type of roles to go after. Now, how in the heck do you find a client? It's really not as hard as you would think. Especially, if you've already established that you've got some sales skills, are good on the phone, and are tenacious enough to not stop making the calls needed until you land a contract. There are lots of books, classes, and advice out there on strategies to find clients. But to keep this as simple as possible you're going to plan your next few weeks, and the hours in your office, on doing nothing but researching companies in your market that are hiring, and making phone calls, and sending emails, to the right people to try and land that job order. The answer to How to find your clients involves the action items. You're going to be 'dialing for dollars' and start building relationships.

What makes someone a good recruiter, or probably a good whatever in any industry, is the awareness that the relationship counts more than the transaction. So, although you are starting with the idea that you want to land a contract to get paid, you really have to sit back and understand the bigger purpose in this time, is going to be to teach you some life lessons. And if you master these lessons, you can master relationships better, and eventually master the money! Baby steps. But great recruiters enjoy and care about the person on the other end of the phone, more than the paycheck a successful relationship will provide. My clients became my friends. At the end of the day, I wanted to help them hire a team of great people, or that one great CEO that will change the life of the company. And on the candidate side, when we speak more to that in Chapter 3, you'll realize that you are going to change these people's lives, and for the better. You are offering them an upgrade in life. You are an agent of change for your candidate and clients, and you want to be a force of good in this world, right?

Too many people would sell their mother for a million dollars-we have enough bad in the world. You get to offer something good, and get paid to do so, because you really care. It's no accident I worked in the medical industry, and later clean technology market. If you're going to pick your sandbox to play in, take a look around this big world, and play in the box that's going to make a difference. So, just please consider me your personal inspirational coach as you go on this journey, because God knows you're going to need one. I never prayed as much as I did when I started my business, but it was one of the best times of my life.

So, let's get to it. To get a job order, you've got to build relationships with the people that can give them to you. That takes you having the right questions prepared for your important call with that person. This is part of your elevator speech we'll discuss further.

How to Get Clients
Developing a Target List of Companies

You'll also need a list of companies you're calling each day, and a way to database all your efforts. I've used many database systems over the years- Goldmine, ACT, Salesforce, Filemaker, Bullhorn, among others. Even being creative with Outlook or other simpler formats can work. You'll just need a way to track your contacts, both clients, and candidates.

You are going to feel like you're "dialing for dollars" for hours, days, and weeks at a time, until you get a hit. If you ever did telemarketing in college, or did tough sales jobs, you'll be more prepared of what to expect. As you get better, so will your odds, so don't be afraid to make mistakes. Just pick up the phone, and start making contacts, which later will lead to contracts. Be sure to utilize LinkedIn as you go, and try to build that network as you make contacts, as that website is a goldmine to recruiters!

Developing Your Elevator Speech

You'll need an "Elevator Speech". This is the 2 minute speech you're going to give when you get the Human Resource Manager, or Hiring Manager on the phone. They call it an elevator speech in sales, because it's figuring out how to concisely state your message within the time you would speak to someone on an elevator. This actually came in very handy during my pharmaceutical sales days, as I did give a lot of sales pitches in the hospital elevators, literally. So, you'll want to have this written down in the beginning, and I can show you an example with one attached, but the idea is to never sound staged. It must read very natural, and after the first dozen or so times, you'll be able to throw it out. Now keep in mind, you may want to actually save those old elevator speeches even after you no longer need them, because as you grow your business, and take on many clients, you may have 10 different elevator speeches for 10 different positions, and you'd be surprised how they can get confusing. So, it's better to file them somewhere for quick access when needed. Like I spoke about on the video session, there are tons of wannabe recruiters calling to get job orders -- what makes you different?

Using your Elevator speech

The actual phone call! This is where most training manuals or books fall short. No one seems to disclose exactly how to make these calls and what to say. These are the details you'll want to be mentored on extensively. This is the stuff you would pick up in an office, but you may only be as successful as the best recruiter in that office that you're able to watch or be taught by. This is where mentoring is key. Having someone who has done this before show you the ropes, and give you insights that may normally have taken you years to learn is worth gold, because it saves you years of time! And contrary to most beliefs, time is more precious than money. Let me cover some of the key points when speaking to a new potential client for the first time.

First, keep it Simple. Second, keep it Short. Third, leave a good impression. Finally, get the details needed and wrap it up. I know this sounds very simplified, but having been the person on the other end of the phone when multiple recruiters would call me wanting to work my jobs- I speak from experience. You want to introduce yourself, and have something to quickly offer that person to make you worth their precious time. If you are calling a Hiring Manager or HR Recruiter wanting to work on a job you found out that they have open- you better come to the table with something from the get go. It makes your call so much more interesting than the others that come in wanting to talk about how they'll do a good job. Make your first call showing them how you are already doing a good job. Keep the call light, gathering some quick information, gain the email or best contact info and ask if you can submit a candidate you have for a specific job that they are working.

Attached are worksheets and checklists to help you get comfortable. But this is also the topic that you'll want to be discussing live time with your mentor! Your major goal this week, in addition to getting your office set up properly- is to be on the phone practicing your Job Order Calls.

Cold Calling Basics

Okay- Let's move onto your first cold call.....Ooooh- scary moment! I still get nervous thinking about those first calls, and I was a seasoned sales professional! You'll be nervous on the first few, but it will get easier, and the time will come soon when you catch yourself giving your "elevator speech" flawlessly for the 30th time, and its working! You'll see- just hang in there until you pass that wall!

After the first couple days of reviewing materials, watching the webinars and getting to know your Recruiting Mentor- You will be alone at your desk trying to figure out the next step. You could spend weeks organizing your office, preparing for the jobs, reviewing techniques, and spend months simply preparing for what you need to start doing today- Make some cold calls. Get your feet wet- Ask your mentor for advice. Put a strategy together of who you're targeting- Find the phone numbers and start 'dialing for dollars.'

Cold Calling

Cold calling is a numbers game, but it can be a lot less tedious when you stack the cards in your favor. Since I was a HR Director and Recruiting Manager for a company before starting my own Recruiting business, I can tell you as good as anyone what companies look for in a recruiter. And the one thing I never had time for were recruiters calling me trying to obtain job orders. I thought they were all the same- they over promised and under delivered. And when I finally would find or take the time to return a call, I was always surprised of how so many would waste my time, and not even ask the necessary questions they should be getting from me on that first call- I guess they didn't know that this may be the one and only time we spoke- so they should have gotten it right! I'm very grateful I had the experience to play the role of HR Manager before I became a recruiter myself. I think it was invaluable experience that helped me differentiate myself form the millions of other recruiters when speaking to a company for the first time.

Do's & Don'ts of Cold Calling

First, you should really never make a "cold call". At best it should be warm, and if you can, it should be hot from the get go. What do I mean by this? Here's a cold call from a recruiter I don't know-

They call- say who they are, from what firm- try to explain how they are different from other recruiting companies, ask about our hiring process, how much do we pay in fees, and want to know about the openings and timelines, blah, blah, blah.

All is well and good, but as a busy HR Director or as busy as any Recruiting Manager would be when trying to fill tons of openings- I did not have time to have these conversations all day- repeating myself and how we work- doing a new contract, and wait to see if they were any good. The recruiters that stood apart were the ones who called not as a typical cold call- but the recruiters who seemed to add value from that first conversation- the ones that made the first call a little 'warmer' by asking all the right questions, and sometimes even leading the call with a resume of someone I may have been interested in. You should be able to know what opening the companies have even before you speak to them- I'll discuss this later. But then, you can email the HR person or Hiring Manager a resume to review (minus the contact info), making your email the cold call, and your live phone call more of a warm follow up. I also found that emailing some company background, website, and referencing other clients was nice to do in email before my conversation, so I wasn't wasting the valuable phone time on 'selling myself and my company'. Similarly to how you will learn to pre-sell your candidate to your client, you are also pre-selling yourself before that first call.

If I was referred to a company from a candidate or colleague- I could often make my first call a 'hot call' to where I not only had candidates to discuss, but could also go after other openings and close an exclusive contract within that first call.

So, to now focus on the basics. Review the job order form, and have that in front of you when you're on the phone with the client so you're asking the right questions. After the questions- you want to set realistic expectations.

Let's review goals from week 1 &2 now since some of this is from week 1, and there was much more to learn here in week 2. It's easy to keep on reading thru the chapters without doing the work, but I would encourage you to take this time to make sure you are checking things off the list, before the tasks seem overwhelmning!

Job Orders

Getting the job order is often thought to be the toughest part of recruiting. Others might say that finding the right candidate is the hardest part of recruiting. Both are true. Getting the job order is half the work, and then finding the candidate is the other part. This is why many recruiters do "splits." If you find the job order, and outsource finding the candidate, you can often split the fee.

In my experience, there will be times when job orders are plenty, and you would happily give away half of the 10, 15 or 30k fee to quickly get the right person for the job. At other slow times, and every recruiter has them- especially if you try to stay in the exclusive or retained realm. There will be times when good job orders seem slim, but you have a million good candidates. To be successful, you'll have to get good at doing both, and know how to ride the fast times, the slow times, and the plateaus you will experience in recruiting.

Your first week, and second, and every week from this week forward will consist of you spending specified days soliciting job orders. You can choose a couple of hours each day to dedicate to this, certain days of the week or both- but you need to start making this a habit you get into as you start your journey of becoming a recruiter.

Back-story on Getting Job Orders & Managing Expectations

I use to say that finding job orders were a dime a dozen, and that finding the candidate was the only hard part. But looking back, and after working in 2 industries- I realized I spoke to soon. In medical, I had more jobs than I could handle, and that's when I made that statement many times to many friends. And since I had an established network, and I always seemed to know someone that the HR person or manager knew, I luckily gained instant credibility which must have helped a lot more than I realized at the time.

When I decided to move out of Medical and into the Clean Technology Industry, I thought it would be just as easy, but I was humbled by how long it took me to land my first contract. This was also in the winter of 2008, when economy started tanking, so it definitely took me a bit longer to land my first contract, and I felt like a big loser. So, don't forget the power of an established network. Hiring in an industry where you already have proven yourself and have friends and contacts saves you tons of time, and shortens your ramp up periods.

I'd say, within 3-6 months, you'll have solid clients if you're from the industry, and if you're new, it could take 6-12 months. Sorry, I'm an impatient girl, and I know that sounds like forever, and there are exceptions to the rule. But, in my experience, and even for someone that was accustom to being the first to get a sale, and the youngest "rookie of the year winner" at my first sales jobs out of college...when you're working for yourself, landing a client goes to a whole new level, and you will feel humbled at how long it can take! When I use to sell for GE Medical or GE Capital, I didn't realize how much instant "clout" and credibility that gave me at the time. When I went to a smaller company, I couldn't lean on that, and when I'm representing my own company, it's even tougher to get people to trust you and take a chance on you. If I were you, I'd plan to stay in the same industry thru out this recruiting career, if you want long term profits to come a little easier. At least while you stay in a recruiter role. Becoming a Consultant can help you blur those lines more, and make profits thru different industry markets.

Looking back, I made the move because I was a bit bored, and taking the money for granted. Plus, I just wanted to travel to some new places, and since I made a fast climb in Medical, I didn't really think it would be a hard jump. It was. It took almost a full year to get my own first contract. I was still working my CEO's contract for splits, but after coming from my own business where I got 100% of the profits, my first check was laughable. I suppose I forgot how many times you can split a $100k deal. 50% of 50% after 25% goes to the house is a much smaller percentage! But, my reasons for shifting weren't really about the money at that point. I just came off my best year ever, where SalesSource had made over three times what I was used to, and I just wanted something new and exciting.

I suppose I should have re-set my expectations going into some new market, but $10k a month was my typical standard goal. Even today, it's still a nice number to have coming in per month one way or another. If you're able to be smart with investing and buying some real estate during your initial years of high profits, those rents can later help you hit your monthly nut, whatever that may be, so your time at a desk will hopefully decrease in time....if that's what you want?

Now a days, I've changed the financial expectations, as well as my happiness expectations in order to reset priorities and have more time with my kids. Luckily there's always creative ways to find passive income. As mentioned, rental properties are a great way to start sinking some of your new found money, as well as creative business endeavors. Today, I get paid to be a consultant as a business developer, and just staring to get paid to write, and to mentor again. So, figure out what your monthly nut is, and then you can do the math backwards to get there, maintaining realistic expectations as you go.

More backstory on getting job orders & personal tips. When I first started learning how to find new jobs, I thought I had discovered a great secret. I was basically on a candidate search for a Sales Manager, and of course as I was talking to other Sales Managers, they got to know me and asked me about finding them some sales reps. Although this was not a strategy of mine in the beginning, it did become on thru out the rest of my recruiting career. And of course, as I worked and consulted with other recruiting firms, it seems they all had learned that trick. Usually, similar to my story, the owner or CEO found out the natural way, and then taught this to his team. How cool to stumble upon job openings while searching for other client's positions. Once that light bulb goes off, like in this example, you'll find easier ways to get the job order as you go along. And one day, with any luck, you'll have to turn jobs down because you're running at full capacity!

So, yes, in this example, I would sometimes call Managers under the pretense of offering a job, when in fact I would be fishing for their companies recent openings. This would only work if I did in fact have another position to discuss with them- at least for me. I know many recruiters who can bluff their way thru, but since I don't want to ever have to remember what I say to who, I keep it 100% legitimate, even if I do have a second, more important agenda to my calls! That's worked for me, and I think you will find keeping things clean cut to be the best path as well.

Times will come where you may have 2 or more job orders for the same type of positions. We call this "double dipping". This is a beautiful thing because you do the same amount of work, and can make 2 placements. I'll speak more on this later, and how you can seek these situations out. Okay, onto other ways of finding your first job! We've scoured the job boards, made phone calls, network thru our current contacts- so what else? Well, there are other sites I've used like www.Split it.com, where you share the job, or other networking sites like LinkedIn, or numerous recruiting sites- but to be honest, I've never gone past the job boards, and networking thru my own contacts to find my jobs. My guess is that if you're doing these things right- you won't have to.

Now having said that, everyone finds their own path. Perhaps your first day- you have luck on Craigslist finding a small company looking for an independent recruiter, and never look back. And there are many lists recruiters buy to cold call from. Hopefully, some of your other mentors can share different methods, as I'm sure there's more than one way to get to the go, but for now, I'm going to focus on the methods I have found successful. Using the job boards, and Networking thru current contacts. I believe this is where most recruiting seminars fall short- they never seem to quite get deep enough to show you 'exactly' how to land that job- right down to what you say, and how you say it. When you call, and who you speak to. Expectations you do and don't set, and how to land the Grade A job order thru a Grade A Contract.

Thru all of this be sure to set realistic expectations when it comes to how many calls to land a job order. It could be hundreds or more. But if it takes all week, so what? It should be when, not if. It will happen, just be sure to have realistic expectations so you don't get discouraged after a morning of calls that seem to go nowhere. This is where a mentor is so important.

Mentors

Since I probably won't personally be able to mentor you thru these times, be sure to find a good mentor as you go down this path. I hope to have the NAHBR website set up to also help you connect with the right mentor. This is also the purpose of the back-story sections of this book.

Mentors, and their back-story, offer real world advice because they have lived it. They can help validate what you are feeling and tell you a few of their own war stories to help make you feel not so alone. If you were going to be in an office setting, you could probably find someone there to take you under their wing. However, since I'm talking to many of the Mom's out there who are looking to do this on their own, from their home base, having a mentor is crucial to your success. You need to build a network. Talk to other recruiters. Find the ones that you look up to, that have built a successful recruiting business from home, and make those your teachers. And at the same time, don't forget to help those behind you that are coming up the ranks.

This is what NAHBR will ideally evolve into. At first, it was a simple website for Moms wanting to learn the business, and a place where they could find mentors (which was only myself and another Recruiting Entrepreneur.) As life has progressed, we opened up the site to be a purely networking site for other "Headhunting Housewives" to connect. Now, with LinkedIn helping people connect faster than a web search, NAHBR, the National Association of Home Based Recruiters has become an open group for anyone wanting to learn about home based recruiting. Although you may be recruiting from home while in your shorts, or even by your pool, you always want to maintain your professional connections. Both to your customers, and to use professional networks to keep you connected to the corporate world.

My Back-story on Mentors

Every mentor I had in my Recruiting Career seemed to advance me two or more years ahead. Multiple CEO's that I've gotten to know and admire, and who've become dear friends, have also progressed my career by years. The best part is all the freedom that the money provides, and the experiences you gain during the process. Not only do you save so much time by not trying to figure things out all by yourself, but your relationships in the business often evolve into amazing experiences. Conferences and meetings take place at very cool locations and venues around the country, or even around the world. Conferences at beautiful resorts, meetings on yachts, chats by the pool, celebrations on the beach, annual meetings at lake homes, summer time chats by the ocean, or all-expense paid company trips to the Caribbean. It all becomes such a true blessing, all because of people giving their time to help someone else move up quicker. Thank you to Sharon Mengel and Vince Alcarese who were my first true mentors at GE. They taught me to make sure I use business to increase my quality of life, and not to just let the business, or corporations use me. It can be a great synergy when done right!

It's important for us, as I recount the people that guided me and helped me get here, to remember their contributions. It's easy to lose sight of the people that helped you conquer your own personal mountain, once you're standing at the top. And, we're so quick, to already start setting our aspirations to new mountains, before looking back and reviewing how we got there.

Yes, numbers are easier to point to as bench marks of success on one's career, but it's really the people that made those numbers grow. And yes, numbers do come in very handy when you want to determine at which point will you call yourself successful? Yet, at other times, it may not even be about the numbers at all. It's how you helped someone or made a difference in someone's life.

A balance of both seems ideal, as nothing speaks to the mind as hard numbers and dollars you can put to work for you, but nothing feeds the heart as much as the relationships you developed and the pieces you gave of yourself to the contacts you made along the way. Plus, by having some written out goals, whether it be a dollar amount, or spreading goodwill, when you hit that goal, you can always have reasons to celebrate. Be sure to reward yourself, and others, for a job well done!

Besides, remember that even though you think the million dollar check is the end game...I know a few too many people that hit those goals, and end up a bit lonely, and bored. They cannot recapture old glories, and without building on the relationships, and only focusing on the transaction, life ends up empty instead of full. Start with the end in mind, so you know the money is not the end game. Even the stuff you buy with it is only for a time, and obviously means nothing without loved ones to share it with. Use it to make a difference. Use your time to build something good and lasting. This is what all my good mentors taught me along the way. And that's why every day is fun, and this road rarely feels like work!

Okay, let's get you back to getting your goals in place, and landing that first job, so you can make some good stuff happen. Having paid homage to the mentors who help, I know you're going to need the numbers and dollar signs to feel validated in this new career!

Run the Numbers, Set your Goals, Work Backwards

Basing things off of my own experience, let's start with a goal of at least one a month, and only at the sales rep level- you can earn a fantastic income and have the home and work life balance most people only dream of. I lived in that spot for many years, and it seemed to be the right balance. Especially if you're a mom with a growing family and a big life outside this business you're starting up.

Let's also step back to finding your niche. We talked a lot about it this chapter, but have your made a decision, or written it all down yet? Decide this week- and make some test calls to see if that market is strong. If you are, or were a nurse, try placing nurses for hospitals. If you have an IT background- try to break into that arena to help hire colleagues. Decide on "the who" now. Then research on your computer to make a target list of companies to call.

Setting Realistic Expectations: Under Sell, Over Deliver

Another golden rule at this stage of the game is to always set expectations low and deliver high. Keep in mind this is the "courting" or "dating period" between you and this new client. These rules of engagement will also be mirrored during the dating period between your candidate and client, which will last from the first introduction thru the first few months of employment. We'll discuss this at that time, but the system and thought process will be the same.

Think about when you're getting to know someone, and how when someone does something that is better than expected, how much of an impression this leaves on you. Set yourself up for success this way. If you think the search will take you 3 days to forward your first resume, tell them to expect candidates the following week. And once you're in the door with a client, getting job order 2, and 4, and 20, don't let their training deadline pressures compromise your recruiting process.

If it's Monday, and they want to put a person in training Friday-don't make promises you can't keep. The truth of the Recruiting Process, at least in my industry, is that it's truly a 6- 8-12 week process. I'll discuss this more later, but I think you'll find the same to be true in any recruiting process. The process typically includes a phone interview, a face to face interview, a final interview, the acceptance and a 2 week notice. It will usually take at least 6-8 or 12 weeks from the time you get the order until an offer letter is signed and you have an official "start date."

The start date becomes all important as that's the date you would typically invoice from, and remember you won't actually get paid until usually net 30 from the start date, so you'll need a nice flowing pipeline of jobs to continue the cash flow. Keep in mind, these time frames are very different if you're hiring temporary help, or hiring a CEO. The temp can be transferred within weeks, and the CEO, although you may find and have her in process within the first 6-8 weeks, it usually takes another 4-8 for flights across the country, and setting a start date in future that makes for a clean exit. My timelines are flexible, but remained a good rule of thumb whether I was hiring C-Level, or sales guys.

Number Games

Now, just like cold calling which is a numbers game, so are the job orders. What I mean is that you'll find that for every 20 or so cold calls you make, you get that one golden, solid job order. And you'll find that the same thing true when going after the candidates to fill your job orders. The number may be different for the different jobs. You may notice 10 phone calls gets you 2 possible leads, and out of the 8 not interested, perhaps they referred you to 4 more leads. It becomes a network that you are building. One phone call leading you to the next one. It can often feel like a web your building, as one call links to the next, especially when you start looking for candidates. This is where referrals are so important, and as I would always say when pumping for referrals, "good people know good people." Plus, although most people want to help for free, I would offer $1k for referrals I placed that year, and I loved sending unexpected $1000 dollar checks around the holidays to people who helped me locate someone good for a job!

So, getting back to cold calling, you will find that each call gets easier, and what use to take you days to do when cold calling, you will start to accomplish the same task in hours. You'll see when it makes sense to use phone- when to email- the best way to follow up, and you will get into a rhythm that will eventually lead you to a closed job order- Our big goal of this class!

Back-story on Numbers & Goal Setting

Never forget the main goal for the day. As your mind may tend to race to a million other tasks needed to be done, just stay focused on landing your job order. I have found that most people that find logical excuses to spend time getting their business plans further in place, or meeting the designer to review the business card logo. These people seem to lose momentum by focusing on the wrong priorities at the wrong time. Your goal is to land that first job order as quick as possible, and that could be a few weeks, or sometimes a few months. You'll need this first job order as soon as possible to build confidence that you can do this. If three months go by, and you have a beautiful decorated office, a glossy business plan, and cards, but haven't really closed a deal yet, you're not going to feel that great, and it's easier to give up.

Anybody can do those other mundane tasks, and you can do them yourself at the proper time, but right now you're going to close your first job order, so you start building some of your own successes. And then we're going to celebrate those successes! A business partner of mine use to get a six pack of champagne in a can- I think it's called Sophie. Yeah, I know....real high class stuff, but there was just something about closing a big deal, and breaking out the Sophie on a sunny Thursday afternoon.

Whatever your ritual, plan little celebrations to remind yourself of your accomplishments. You'll have plenty of failures along the way- rude people, unreturned phone calls, candidates pulling out at the last minute or not even showing up. It's not if this will happen, but it's when will this happen to you, so man-up, and be ready, and only judge yourself on how you react to the situation instead of reacting to the situation. All life lessons I'm sure you already know, but things we can always be reminded. This is what good mentors can often offer you. Not only a reminder of some wisdom, but inspiration and laughter to carry you thru the tougher times too.

Now, as you focus on this goal of landing the first job order, many wannabe recruiters can get lost within their own process, and never get to the finish line. They may get lost in the search without focusing attention on the right detail, they may not be able to take the hundreds of rejections for the few approvals they receive. Many of you may spend too much time talking to the clients and talking to the candidates, without the direction needed to get you to your goal.

Remember that your time is precious, and every call and every item you focus on each hour of each day should have the purpose of you filling that job request. Obviously, you'll want to be relaxed and enjoy your conversations, especially with that "A" candidate or any Client that you want to build a relationship with, but be mindful of the clock. And remind yourself of the goal for the day, setting time frames to focus on that goal each day, until you can check off that box, and move onto the candidate side.

So, I think enough on that topic. We're staying focused on our goal this week of closing job orders, so, that makes this week's prime objective to GET that first job order!

Now many recruiters will say, and I've been known to be one of them- that Job orders are a dime a dozen. It's not hard to get a job order because companies love to have recruiters working their jobs and fueling their databases for free, mind you. So don't be one of the suckers that are working for free. There was a time that I considered all contingent recruiters to belong in that league, but then life did humble me when a few of my large exclusive and retained clients were not hiring as many people as they used too, and since I had recruiters working for me, depending on me to bring in the jobs for them to work- I also contracted for brief periods as a contingent recruiter to get thru the slim periods.

I did however minimize my risk by having very clear conversations with the Hiring Manager to be sure there were no more than 1-2 other recruiters on the hunt, and I planted the seed early that my goal was to prove myself so that I could be their exclusive recruiter on future jobs- which actually worked out.

Knowing that you'll be starting from scratch- I'm not going to knock contingency contracts, because the more competitive our industry gets, that may be all that is available to you. However, you should keep your eye on the ball, of wanting to make that client exclusive or retained in the future, and that seed should be planted at the first phone call.

You're goal, as we discussed on this day is to make cold calls and get comfortable speaking to companies. You're goal today doesn't have to be landing a contract...For now, the goal is to learn the elevator speech, and get good at making the calls so they become second nature.

Week 2 Checklist

Chapter 2:   Week 2- Find Clients & Get Job Order

- ✓ Review Chap 1- work on items not yet completed.
- ✓ Read Chapter 2
- ✓ Decide on your niche market
- ✓ Develop 'elevator speech' for obtaining contract
- ✓ Start cold calling client companies
- ✓ Do's and Don'ts of Cold Calling
- ✓ Maintain weekly schedule- cold call during scheduled times (3hr time slots)
- ✓ Have at least 20 companies to call per week- Make list

✓ Maintain notes on potential clients in word document

Cold Calling for job orders may take a few weeks to land first one; simply keep the schedule, and it will happen!! Should have 1st job within 5-7 weeks ideally, or by the end this 10 week course*

See attachments:

Contract Examples

Job Order Examples

Job Description Examples

Profile Templates

Elevator speech Examples

Script Templates

Contract Example:

CONTINGENCY SEARCH FIRM AGREEMENT

The following outlines the terms and conditions of the agreement between xxxx Corporation (hereinafter referred to as "xxxx") and _____(hereinafter referred to as the "Firm") regarding the referral by the Firm of candidates for open positions at xxxxx.

1.0   TERM

This Agreement shall commence on _____and remain in full force for one year, unless terminated pursuant to paragraph 13.0 below.

2.0   SERVICES TO BE PROVIDED BY FIRM

2.1   The Firm Hereby agrees to submit resumes/applications only in response to a specific open position that has been brought to its attention by xxxxx (hereinafter the "Open Position"). Accordingly, the Firm understands and agrees that it will not submit any resumes/applications in response to a public advertisement or which were not solicited by xxxxx. Any submission by the Firm must be sent directly to   The submission must specifically note the xxxxx job order number in the subject line of the email message. Resumes may be attached or embedded in the text of the email message. The candidate's name, phone number and/or email address must be displayed on the resume.

2.2   The Firm agrees to provide equal opportunity to all qualified candidates by referring such candidates on the basis of merit and without regard to the candidate's race, color, religion, national origin, sex, age, disability, veteran status, or other characteristic protected by law. The Firm agrees to exercise good faith efforts to find qualified candidates of diverse backgrounds, in particular minorities and females, disabled individuals, and disabled,

Vietnam-era and other eligible (as defined by law) veterans if providing candidates to xxxx in the U.S.

3.0 FEES

3.1 xxxx will pay the Firm a fee equal to _____percent (%) of the base annual salary (the "Placement Fee") of any candidate referred to xxxxand successfully placed within the Open Position to which the candidate was referred in accordance with the provisions of this Agreement. The Firm will submit an invoice for the Placement Fee to xxxxx once the candidate has commenced employment with xxxxx.

3.2 xxxx will not be required to pay a Placement Fee to the Firm if such candidate is hired by xxxxx for any other position than the Open Position and the candidate's resume/application has been received by xxxxx from any other source at any time. If the resume/application has not been received by xxxxx from any other source at any time and the candidate is hired for another position within six months of the date when the candidate's paperwork was first submitted by the Firm xxxxx will pay the Firm in accordance with paragraph 3.1.

3.3 Notwithstanding paragraph 3.1, xxxx will not be required to pay to the Firm a Placement Fee if the candidate referred to xxxby the Firm is a:

a) Former xxxx (or affiliate of xxxx) employee who has been removed from xxxxx payroll for less than two years;

b) recent full-time college graduate (graduation within 24 months of the date the candidate is referred to xxxxx and including but not limited to graduates of Master's, Ph.d. or professional degree programs); or

c) Contract or other non-xxxx worker who is currently working in the business to which the Firm refers the candidate.

4.0 UNSUCCESSFUL PLACEMENT

In the even any candidate referred by the Firm leaves xxxxx or is terminated or any reason (other than due to a business-initiated reduction-in-force) within ninety (90) days of the commencement date of employment, the Firm agrees, at xxxx's discretion, to: a) provide a replacement (who is ultimately hired by xxxxxx) within ninety days, at no additional charge, or b) adjust the amount of fees owed to the Firm by the amount of the Placement Fee.

5.0   COMPETING AGENCIES

5.1   xxxx   agrees   it   will   only   receive   and   enter resumes/applications referred by agencies/search firms into its xxxx-wide database if such Firm has executed this Agreement.

5.2   In the event that xxxx receives resumes/applications concerning the same candidate form two different sources for the Open Position, xxxx will determine which resume was first received by xxxx. The source (e.g., a Firm) who referred the first-received resume/application will be the recipient of the Placement Fee, if such a fee is due under the terms of this Agreement.

6.0   RESTRICTIONS ON SOLICITATION OF xxxx EMPLOYEES

During the term of this Agreement, the Firm agrees that it will not directly or indirectly solicit any person who is am employs of xxxxxx to terminate his/her employment with xxxx, without first obtaining approval to do so from the responsible Human Resources manager for such employee.

7.0   DISCLOSURE OF INFORMATION

7.1   Neither the Firm nor any individual performing services under this Agreement on behalf of the Firm shall, without prior written consent of xxxx, disclose to any person outside of xxxx, or publish, at any time, any xxxxproprietary, confidential or trade secret information which may be obtained by the Firm through the furnishings of services under this Agreement, including but not limited to, information about xxxx its employees, organization, activities, policies or products, and including any reports or data analysis prepared by the Firm in connection with this Agreement.

7.2   xxxx   understands   that   the   information   regarding candidates is provided to xxxx by the Firm for xxxs sole use. Xxxx agrees not to disclose, outside of xxxx and its affiliates, any of the candidate information submitted by the Firm in accordance with paragraph 2.1, without the written consent of the Firm.

7.3   The Firm acknowledges that any personal data transferred to xxxx & subject to the EU Directive 95/46 on Data Protection, as amended from time to time, or as defined in the national data protection rules of all applicable countries, as amended or replaced from time to time, is obtained, held, stored & processed in accordance with the Data Protection Legislation.   The Firm is responsible for obtaining any necessary consents for the data to be transferred & processed by all xxxx affiliates & authorized service providers for the purposes of employment.

8.0   STATUS OF THE FIRM

8.1   The Firm, and any principle, partner, agent or employee of the Firm (hereinafter "Firm Representatives") are independent contractors under this Agreement and will not, by virtue of this Agreement, be considered as employees of xxxx for any purpose, including but not limited to eligibility for xxxx benefits or compensation or other rights and privileges afforded to employees of xxxxx.

8.2   The Firm Representatives will not represent themselves as agents of xxx, will not commit or obligate xxxxx to others in any way, and will not act in a manner which compromises or exposes xxxxx liability to others.

9.0   COMPLIANCE AND GOVERNING LAW

9.1   The Firm agrees to comply with all applicable federal, state, and local laws, regulations, and ordinances in providing the services under this Agreement.

9.2   This Agreement shall be construed, interpreted, and applied in accordance with the law of the State of Maryland.

10.0   BACKGROUND INVESTIGATIONS

xxxxx will be responsible for conducting any background investigations, including but not limited to past employment, educational and criminal history, on all candidates presented to xxxxx.

11.0   ADMINISTRATION OF THE AGREEMENT

Diane O'Brien is hereby designated as xxxx's duly authorized representative for purposes of administration of this Agreement. It is understood and agreed that Diane O'Brien must make all requests for the Firm's services hereunder in order for the services to qualify for payment.   Xxxx may by written notice appoint another xxxx representative forth foregoing purposes.

12.0   INDEMNIFICATION

The Firm shall defend, hold harmless and indemnify xxxxx from and against any and all claims, demands, liabilities, suits, actions, losses, damages, costs, expenses and reasonable attorney's fees arising from the Firm's performance or breach of its obligations under this Agreement.

13.0   TERMINATION

Either party may terminate this Agreement at any time for convenience by sending, via reputable overnight carrier, a written notice of termination to the other party at least 30 days in advance of the date for termination to the address stated at the end of the Agreement. In the event of such termination, the Firm will be paid for all fees due hereunder (including Placement Fees for candidates who are properly referred consistent with Paragraphs 2, 3, and 4 prior to the termination date of the Agreement ("Termination Date") but are not successfully placed until after the Termination Date) up to the date of such termination and not thereafter. Payment upon termination will be accepted by the Firm in full satisfaction of all claims and demands against xxxx based upon or arising out of or in connection with this Agreement. The obligations under Paragraph 12 (Indemnification) herein shall survive the termination of this Agreement.

14.0   ASSESSMENT

Neither this Agreement nor any rights or obligations hereunder may be assigned or otherwise transferred by the Firm without the prior written consent of xxxx.

15.0 NO WAIVER

The waiver of XXXX of any term, covenant or condition herein contained shall not be deemed to be a waiver of any subsequent breach of the same or a waiver of any other term, covenant or condition herein contained. No covenant, term, or condition of this Agreement shall be deemed to have been waived by xxxxx unless such waiver be in writing and executed by xxxx.

15.0   ENTIRE AGREEMENT

This Agreement is the complete, final, and exclusive agreement between the Firm and xxxxx with respect to the referral of qualified candidates to xxxxx, and it supersedes all prior agreements and understandings with respect thereto.

By: _____   By:
_____

Title: _____   Title:
_____

Date: _____   Date:
_____

The following must be completed by the Firm:

Name   of   Firm:
_____
_____

Name   of   Contact   at   Firm:
_____

Area   of   Firm's   specialty:

_____

Address:

_____
_____
(Street Address) (City)   (State)   (Zip Code)

Phone: _____ Fax:

_____

Email: _____

Retained Example (1):

Retained Search Agreement

This Search Agreement is made between COMPANY of address and company, address.

Position(s) exclusively retained for Searches:

Total Search Fee: Is equal to 33 1/3% of the candidate's first year's guaranteed income (to include bonuses, sign-on or projected incentive bonus payment)

Retainer: A retainer fee of $16,500 is due to initiate the search. xxxx's Performance Guarantee: This retainer is fully refundable within 60 days if you are not satisfied with the candidates presented.
Second Payment: A second installment of $16,500 is due once selected candidate(s) is/are scheduled to interview; typically 30 days after initiation of search.

Final payment: The retainer and installment fees will be applied and subtracted from the final total fee for the placement. The cash balance will be earned upon completion of the search and due upon the placed candidate's starting date.

Guarantee Period: 6 months replacement (contingent on timely payment of invoice)

This search is exclusive. The fee applies to any applicant referred by us for a specified position or an alternate position offered and employed by you within a one year period from the date of referral. During the term of this agreement, we will act as your exclusive recruiting agent for positions falling within the scope of the agreement. If, during the term of this agreement, any potential candidates for these positions should come to your attention from any other referral sources, they will be referred to us for screening in the same manner as potential candidates identified by us.

You give us your full cooperation. This includes providing comprehensive information on what you expect a successful candidate to have in the way of experience and qualifications, and a complete and accurate job description, including pay and benefits. This also includes making all personnel involved in the search available for telephone conferences and candidate interviews as necessary to ensure the successful completion of the search within the agreed to time frame.

We guarantee our performance. We guarantee that any candidate you hire under the terms of this agreement will not leave voluntarily or be discharged due to misconduct or good cause (misconduct or unsatisfactory performance determined according to reasonable standards) during the guarantee period. However, our guarantee does not apply if the termination is a result of a layoff, elimination of the position, a substantial change in the job description or reporting structure, a change in your ownership, or any other reason beyond the candidate's control. If the candidate does voluntarily leave or is discharged for good cause during the guarantee period, we will repeat the search process for no additional fees. This is your exclusive remedy under our guarantee. You will not be entitled to any refund of fees or costs, and xxxx shall not be liable for compensatory or other damages resulting from the employment of the candidate.

You guarantee your performance. If you cancel the search before the exclusive period is over, without making a hiring decision, we will consider any payments made to be payment in full for our services. Should you significantly change the position, responsibilities, or job description, a new agreement must be signed and an additional retainer must be paid. If you hire a candidate referred by xxxxx within one (1) year of our referral, for any position with your company or with any subsidiary, affiliate or related company, you are obliged to pay xxxx the total search fee as stated above.

Important: You need to keep your guarantees active. Our guarantees to you will remain active for as long as you abide by this Agreement. All that is required is our receipt of the final payment of the search fee as agreed to in the above schedule and notification within two (2) business days of the candidate's last day of work if they are terminated.

COMPANY: For xxxxx :

_____   _____

Client   Date
                        Date

Other Contract Examples (2):

Terms and Conditions Contingency Recruitment Services (Form A)

WHEREAS, the Contract is entered into effective as of the date indicated in the body of the Purchase Document between Supplier and Purchaser; and

WHEREAS, Purchaser desires to engage Supplier from time to time for the performance of Recruiting Services, and Supplier is willing to perform such Recruiting Services on the terms and conditions set forth below; and

WHEREAS, all Recruiting Services will be performed pursuant to the terms of the Contract unless the Parties agree in writing that the Recruiting Services are of a type that should be the subject of a separate agreement containing appropriate terms and conditions to be agreed upon by the Parties; and

WHEREAS, Supplier desires to provide the Recruiting Services under the Contract and represents that it is qualified to perform such Recruiting Services.

NOW, THEREFORE, in consideration of the mutual covenants and agreements set forth in the Contract, and for other good and valuable consideration, the receipt and sufficiency of which are hereby acknowledged, the Parties agree as follows:

1.0 Definitions:

When used in these Terms and Conditions for contingency recruitment Services (Form A) with initial or complete capitalization, whether in singular or in plural, the following terms have the following defined meanings:

1.1 Base Salary: Equals Candidate's annual salary less any bonuses, incentives, merit or other pay adders.

1.2 Candidate: A competent worker who meets the technical and/or professional qualification requirements as specified by the Recruiter for the Candidate Position identified in the Purchase Document.

1.3 Change Order Form: A signed Purchaser form which serves as an amendment to the Contract and which may include changes in the scope of Recruiting Services.

1.4 Contingency: Describes the relationship between the Parties, whereby Supplier's services are reimbursed contingent upon Purchaser's acceptance and direct hire of the Supplier sourced and/or referred Candidate.

1.5 Contingent Fee: The placement fee Supplier is entitled under the Contract, which shall be calculated as a percentage of Candidate's first year Base Salary as stipulated in Section 3.1 of this Contract.

1.6 Contract: The agreement between Purchaser and Supplier as set forth in (i) the body of the Purchase Document; (ii) these Terms and Conditions for Contingency Recruitment Services (Form A); (iii) other documents as may be incorporated into the Purchase Document such as supplemental terms and conditions, specifications, and schedules; and (iv) any subsequent Change Order Forms.

1.7 Parties: Purchaser and Supplier.

1.8 Purchase Document: The Purchaser purchase order, purchase order release or purchase contract form that is a part of and incorporates the remaining documents comprising the Contract.

1.9 Parties: Purchaser and Supplier.

1.10 Recruiter: The Purchaser Human Resources representative responsible for admin.

1.11 Purchaser: The legal entity named and designated as the Purchaser on the Purchase Document.

1.12 Purchaser Entities: Purchaser, its parent, subsidiaries and any affiliated company of xxx Energy, Inc. (and its successors and assigns) and their respective officers, directors, agents and employees.

1.13 Party: Purchaser or Supplier of recruiting and staffing on behalf of Purchaser. Supplier shall contact the Purchaser procurement representative or the Purchaser Company Representative identified in the Purchase Document to identify such individual in such case as none is identified on the Purchase Document.

1.14 Recruiting Services: Any recruitment management services and activities necessary for the execution and timely completion of Supplier's obligations under the Contract including, but not limited to, the activities which may be set forth in Section 2.0, Scope of Work, or a proposal for Recruiting Services, or in the body of the Purchase Document.

1.15 Supplier: The individual or organization responsible for performing the work as identified in the reference Purchase Document

2.0 Scope of Work:

2.1 Supplier shall perform all activities necessary to source and directly refer Candidate(s) suitable for filling Purchaser's hiring requirements. Purchaser is in no way obligated to hire any of the Candidates referred by Supplier hereunder. Supplier shall source and/or refer only those Candidates in direct response to Purchaser hiring requirements as identified by the Recruiter.

2.2 Purchaser's obligation for payment of the Contingency Fee under the Contract shall only extend for a period of six (6) months 1year from the date of Candidate submittal by Supplier to the Recruiter for those Candidates that Purchaser has not previously sourced for a position at Purchaser within six (6) months of said submittal of said potential Candidate by Supplier to the Recruiter. Where Purchaser has previously sourced the Candidate submitted by the Supplier to the Recruiter, Purchaser will endeavor to provide notice as to refusal of such Candidate to Supplier within thirty (30) days.

2.3 The parties agree and acknowledge that Purchaser will not be held liable for payment of a Contingency Fee where a Candidate referral is not directed to the designated Recruiter.

2.4 Changes in the scope of this Contract, including any and all modifications, changes and/or additions to the Recruiting Services, will only be performed when authorized by a Change Order Form.

2.5 If within the first ninety (90) days of the Candidate's employment with Purchaser, the Candidate leaves or is terminated for any reason other than reorganization or layoff by Purchaser, Supplier shall provide a suitable replacement Candidate within fifteen (15) business days or refund the Contingency Fee, provided Purchaser provides Supplier notification of the resignation or termination and reasons for it within ten (10) business days of such date that Candidate leaves or is otherwise terminated.

3.0 Invoicing and Payment:

3.1 Purchaser agrees to pay Supplier a Contingent Fee of twenty two and a half percent (22 ½%) of the Candidate's first year Base Salary, unless otherwise specified in the Purchase Document.

3.2 Purchaser's payment terms are Net 45, based upon receipt of a correct invoice unless otherwise identified in the Purchase Document. Supplier may bill Purchaser following Candidate's employment start date with Purchaser. Purchaser's aggregate liability is limited to the Contingency Fee for Purchaser hired Candidates only.

3.3 Invoices must include the Purchase Document number and Candidate's name. Incorrect invoices will be returned to Supplier. Corrected invoices will be re-dated and retransmitted.

3.4 The Contingency Fee is due and payable only if Candidate becomes an Purchaser hire on a full-time basis (i) for the open position that Supplier originally submitted Candidate's name, and (ii) within six (6) months of the most recent communication between Purchaser and Supplier relating to said Candidate.

4.0 Order of Interpretation:

In case of conflict between or among documents related to this Contract, the following order of precedence shall apply unless otherwise specified: first: Change Order Forms; second: information contained in the body of the Purchase Document; third: these Terms and Conditions for Contingency Recruiting Services; fourth: any attached supplemental terms and conditions referenced in the Purchase Document; and fifth: other documents such as specifications and schedules.

5.0 Confidentiality AND NON-SOLICITATION:

5.1 Any materials and information belonging to or in the possession of Purchaser and provided or otherwise disclosed to Supplier, including the terms and conditions of the Contract, whether written, printed or otherwise recorded, as well as all work products resulting from the Contract (collectively, "Purchaser

Confidential Information"), shall be used by Supplier only in the performance and duties hereunder and Supplier shall not record, reference, reproduce or use such materials for any other purpose without the express written consent of Purchaser. All rights, title to and interest in any Purchaser Confidential Information shall remain with Purchaser, and all such Purchaser Confidential Information shall be returned to Purchaser immediately upon termination of this Contract, or any time prior thereto, upon the request of Purchaser.

5.2 Neither Party shall release any information concerning this Contract, make any announcements except as may be required by law, to any third Party, member of the public, press or official body, unless prior written consent is obtained from both Parties.

5.3 This Section 5.0 does not apply to information that is presently a matter of public knowledge or which is published in or otherwise obtainable from any source available to the public without a breach of the Contract by the Supplier or its personnel. Supplier's obligations under this Section 5.0 will also not apply to any of the following: (i) information already known to Supplier at the time of disclosure; (ii) information available to Supplier from third parties without any nondisclosure obligation to Purchaser that is known or reasonably should have been known to Supplier; or (iii) information independently developed by Supplier without the aid of Purchaser-provided Confidential Information. If any court or regulatory order or other service of legal process requires Supplier to disclose information covered by Supplier's confidentiality obligation, then Supplier may make any disclosure required by law. Supplier will provide Purchaser with prompt notice of any such order or process and cooperate with Purchaser in responding to the order or process.

5.4 During the term of the Contract and one (1) year after the termination or expiration of the Recruiting Services performed under the Contract, Supplier shall not without prior consent directly solicit for employment (whether as an employee, contractor, or agent) any employee of Purchaser Entities.

6.0 Warranty:

6.1 Supplier represents and warrants to Purchaser that the Contract has been duly and validly authorized, executed and delivered and is the legal, valid and binding obligation of the Supplier, enforceable in accordance with its terms.

6.2 Supplier further represents and warrants that the execution, delivery and performance of the Contract are not events which of themselves or, with the giving of notice or the passage of time or both, would constitute, on the part of Supplier, a violation of, or conflict with, or result in a breach of, or default under, the terms, conditions or provisions of (i) any order, writ, injunction, decree, judgment, law or regulation, or (ii) any agreement or instrument to which Supplier is a party or by which it is bound. Supplier further represents and warrants that the execution, delivery and performance of the Contract will not result in a conflict of interest with respect to Supplier's obligations to any other party.

6.3 If during the course of performing the Recruiting Services, Supplier becomes aware of any potential conflict of interest, Supplier shall so notify Purchaser promptly in writing. For purposes of this Section 6.3, "conflict of interest" means the occurrence of any personal interest of Supplier (whether direct or indirect) where Supplier has either given or received or has appeared to have given or received any unfair advantage or preferential treatment not available to others in connection with the Recruiting Services under the Contract. Supplier represents and warrants that neither Supplier will give (or receive or authorize, offer or promise to give) payment or anything of value, either directly or indirectly, to or from any person not a Party to the Contract the receipt of which (i) is or may be intended for the purposes of rewarding, inducing or influencing or (ii) rewards, induces or influences an act, decision or recommendation in connection with the performance of the Recruiting Services or any counsel thereunder. For the purposes of the foregoing sentence, the phrase "anything of value" includes, but is not limited to, the receipt or promise of commissions, financial or ownership interests, assistance in obtaining or retaining business for or with Supplier, and assistance in directing business to any person.

6.4 Supplier shall perform the Recruiting Services under the Contract with the degree of knowledge, skill and judgment customarily exercised by professional firms with respect to services of a similar nature, in a workman-like manner according to generally accepted standards of the temporary workforce management industry and in accordance with all applicable laws, rules and regulations.

7.0 Equal Employment Opportunity And Civil Rights

Supplier shall conform to the requirements of the Equal Employment Opportunity clause in Section 202, Paragraphs 1 through 7, of Executive Order 11246, as amended, and applicable portions of Executive Orders 11701 and 11758, relative to Equal Employment Opportunity and the Implementing Rules and Regulations of the Office of Federal Contract Compliance Programs, and shall impose these requirements upon applicable subcontractors.

8.0 Termination for Cause and Convenience:

8.1 Each Party may, upon written notice to the other Party, and without prejudice to any remedy available to such Party under law, in equity or under the Contract, terminate the whole or any part of the Contract without termination charge, penalty or obligation in the event a Party fails to perform a material obligation under the Contract and fails to cure such material obligation default within a commercially reasonable period of time, but in no event more than thirty (30) days after written notice from the non-breaching Party specifying the nature of such default.

8.2 Purchaser shall have the right to terminate this Contract for its convenience in whole or in part at any time, upon ten (10) days' written notice to Supplier. Should Purchaser elect to terminate the Contract under this Section 8.2, complete settlement of all claims of Supplier arising thereunder shall be made as follows: (i) Purchaser shall compensate Supplier for such Recruiting Services performed after the date written notice is given only as approved in advance by Purchaser; and (ii) Purchaser shall pay Supplier for that portion of the Recruiting Services actually completed in accordance with the terms of the Contract. Supplier shall take all reasonable steps to minimize termination charges, costs and liability with respect to terminated Recruiting Services. At its option, Purchaser may conduct an audit of Supplier's records to verify that termination charges are reasonable and proper. Payment of such charges identified in this Section 8.2 shall be Purchaser's sole obligation and Supplier's exclusive remedy for termination for convenience.

9.0 independent Contractor:

Supplier agrees to perform Recruiting Services as an independent contractor and not as a subcontractor, agent or employee of Purchaser, its parent, subsidiaries or affiliates. Purchaser retains no control or direction over Supplier, its employees or over the detail, manner or methods of performance of Recruiting Services. Supplier is not granted any right or authority or responsibility expressed, implied or apparent on behalf of or in the name of Purchaser to bind or act on behalf of Purchaser.

10.0 Taxes:

Supplier is responsible for and shall pay all taxes due under the Contract, if any, including all present applicable state sales and use taxes and all present or future import duty, federal, state, county, municipal or other excise or similar taxes levied with respect to the Recruiting Services unless otherwise set forth in Purchaser's Purchase Document. Supplier expressly agrees that Purchaser shall incur no liability or expense under this Contract due to change in tax or duty requirements, excluding applicable state sales and use tax. Any increase in taxes or duties, excluding applicable state sales and use tax, shall be at the expense of Supplier and not Purchaser. In no event shall Purchaser be required to pay any tax levied on or determined by Supplier's income, taxes expressly designed to be paid solely by Supplier or licenses and permits required for Supplier to conduct business. Purchaser shall not be obligated to pay, and shall be immediately reimbursed by Supplier if Purchaser does pay, any taxes, including penalties or interest charges levied or assessed by reason of any failure of Supplier to comply with this Contract, applicable laws or governmental regulations, and Supplier shall indemnify and hold Purchaser harmless from the payment of any and all such taxes, penalties and interest.

11.0 Governing law & VENUE:

11.1 Supplier shall comply with all applicable laws, and the Contract shall be construed in accordance with and governed by the laws of the State of Florida, without giving effect to its conflict of laws provisions.

11.2 Any disputes resulting in litigation between the Parties shall be conducted in the state or federal courts of the State of Florida. Proceedings shall take place in the Circuit Court for Miami-Dade County or Palm Beach County, Florida, the United States District Court for the Southern District of Florida, or such other Florida location or forum all at Purchaser's election.

11.3 THE PARTIES TO THE CONTRACT HEREBY KNOWINGLY, VOLUNTARILY, AND INTENTIONALLY WAIVE ANY RIGHT THAT MAY EXIST TO HAVE A TRIAL BY JURY IN RESPECT OF ANY LITIGATION BASED UPON OR ARISING OUT OF, UNDER, OR IN ANY WAY CONNECTED WITH, THE CONTRACT OR THE PERFORMANCE OF recruiting services BY supplier HEREUNDER.

12.0 **Non-waiver:**

No waiver of any Section of the Contract shall be deemed to be nor shall constitute a waiver of any other Section whether or not similar, nor shall any waiver constitute a continuing waiver. No waiver shall be binding unless executed in writing by the Party making the waiver.

13.0 **Survival:**

The obligations of the Parties hereunder which by their nature survive the termination of the Contract and/or the completion of Recruiting Services hereunder shall survive and inure to the benefit of the Parties. Those Sections of the Contract which provide for the limitation of or protection against liability, which includes, without limitation, Sections 5.0, 10.0, and 14.0, shall apply to the full extent permitted by law and shall survive termination of the Contract.

14.0 **Indemnification and Limitation of Liability:**

14.1 Supplier agrees to protect, defend, indemnify and hold Purchaser Entities free and unharmed from and against any liabilities whatsoever resulting from or in connection with the Contract or in connection with performance under this Contract by Supplier, occasioned wholly or in part by the negligence of Supplier.

14.2 In no event shall Purchaser Entities be liable to Supplier, its subcontractors or supplier for indirect, incidental or consequential damages, resulting from Purchaser's performance, nonperformance or delay in performance of obligations under the Contract, or from Purchaser's delay, termination or suspensions of the scope of Recruiting Services under the Contract.

"Exclusive" or "Contained" Example Contracts:

Retained Search Agreement

This Search Agreement is made between xxx and xxxx
Position(s) retained for Searches: Sales Development Manager, North America

Total Search Fee: Is equal to 33 1/3% of the candidate's first year's guaranteed income (to include bonuses, sign-on or projected incentive bonus payment)

Retainer: A retainer fee of $14,500 is due to initiate the search.
XXXX's Performance Guarantee: This retainer is fully refundable within 60 days if you are not satisfied with the candidates presented.
Second Payment: A second installment of $14,500 is due once selected candidate(s) is/are scheduled to interview; typically 30 days after initiation of search.
Final payment: The retainer and installment fees will be applied and subtracted from the final total fee for the placement. The cash balance will be earned upon completion of the search and due upon the placed candidate's starting date.

Guarantee Period: 6 months replacement (contingent on timely payment of invoice)

This search is exclusive. The fee applies to any applicant referred by us for a specified position or an alternate position offered and employed by you within a one year period from the date of referral. During the term of this agreement, we will act as your exclusive 'outside' recruiting agency for positions falling within the scope of the agreement.

You give us your full cooperation. This includes providing comprehensive information on what you expect a successful candidate to have in the way of experience and qualifications, and a complete and accurate job description, including pay and benefits. This also includes making all personnel involved in the search available for telephone conferences and candidate interviews as necessary to ensure the successful completion of the search within the agreed to time frame.

We guarantee our performance. We guarantee that any candidate you hire under the terms of this agreement will not leave voluntarily or be discharged due to misconduct or good cause (misconduct or unsatisfactory performance determined according to reasonable standards) during the guarantee period. However, our guarantee does not apply if the termination is a result of a layoff, elimination of the position, a substantial change in the job description or reporting structure, a change in your ownership, or any other reason beyond the candidate's control. If the candidate does voluntarily leave or is discharged for good cause during the guarantee period, we will repeat the search process for no additional fees. This is your exclusive remedy under our guarantee. You will not be entitled to any refund of fees or costs, and XXXX shall not be liable for compensatory or other damages resulting from the employment of the candidate.

You guarantee your performance. If you cancel the search before the exclusive period is over, without making a hiring decision, we will consider any payments made to be payment in full for our services. Should you significantly change the position, responsibilities, or job description, a new agreement must be signed and an additional retainer must be paid. If you hire a candidate referred by xxxxx within one (1) year of our referral, for any position with your company or with any subsidiary, affiliate or related company, you are obliged to pay XXXX the total search fee as stated above.

Important: You need to keep your guarantees active. Our guarantees to you will remain active for as long as you abide by this Agreement. All that is required is our receipt of the final payment of the search fee as agreed to in the above schedule and notification within two (2) business days of the candidate's last day of work if they are terminated.

Signature, Date _____

Diane O'Brien

Phone: 610-935-4858
Fax: 610-935-4857
dobrien@SalesSourceInc.com

Exclusive Recruiting Agreement

This Recruiting Agreement (hereinafter, "Agreement") is made and entered into as of the
day of , year , by and between SalesSource., a Pennsylvania based search firm (hereinafter, "SS") and
,(hereinafter, **"Client"**).

1.   **Recruitment:** SS will use its best efforts to identify, recruit, pre-screen and present only candidates whose qualifications match the search criteria provided by the **Client.** SS will refer these candidates without regard to race, color, religion, sex, age or national origin. **Client** will provide complete information **exclusively** to SS on hiring specifications, salary, benefits, company history and any additional criteria necessary to begin conducting a successful search.

2.   **Identified Candidates:**   When **Client** accepts a candidate referred by SS, whether by phone, fax or mail, **Client** identifies this candidate as a SS candidate and **Client** agrees to honor such candidate as a SS candidate for a period of two years from the date of referral, thus accepting responsibility for SS's placement fee upon the candidate's starting day of employment with **Client, Client's** affiliates, or any third party to whom **Client** may have referred the SS candidate. If **Client** has previously received the same candidate through another source, it is the **Client's** responsibility to advise SS immediately that the candidate is identified as belonging to a source other than SS.

3.   **Confidentiality:** SS will keep confidential all information provided by **Client** except for use in recruiting qualified candidates during the search process. **Client** agrees that all discussion of

search fees and services is confidential and may not be discussed at any time with any SS candidate without written permission from SS. Further, information about SS candidates must not be divulged to anyone outside **Client's** own company without express permission of SS.

    4.   **Facilitation:** SS will assist **Client** to coordinate interviews with SS candidates including interview, scheduling, preparation and debriefing. SS will also assist as requested with reference checking, offer presentations, contract negotiations, relocation coordination and post-placement follow-up.

5. **Interview Expenses:** **Client** agrees to pay any pre-approved interview expenses including transportation, lodging and meals when interviewing SS candidates. All interview arrangements made by SS must be pre-approved by **Client** prior to being made.

6. **Placement Fee:** If **Client** hires a SS candidate at any time during the two-year referral time, **Client** agrees to pay SS a **one time flat fee** as follows: **$ 17,000; 50% is due within 30 days of candidate's start date; and 50% is due within 90 days of start date.** In the event the **Client** refers the SS candidate to a 3rd party without written approval of SS, and that referral results in the employment of the SS candidate by that 3rd party, **Client** is then responsible for paying SS the placement fee defined in this section.

7.   **Replacement and/or Refund:** If the referred candidate does not commence working for any reason during the first 3 months, SS will assist **Client** to secure a replacement candidate at no additional cost.

    This replacement and/or refund will only be honored if full payment of Placement Fee is paid to SS <u>within 30 days of the candidate's starting date of employment.</u>

8.   **Late Charges and Collection Expenses:** Our charges are paid solely by the **Client** and are due within 30 days of the candidate's starting date of employment. A late charge will be assessed at the rate of 10% per month (12% APR) on all balances remaining unpaid beyond 10 days of the employee's start date. **Client** further agrees that it will be liable for **SS's** expenses

incurred in collecting any placement fee or portion thereof not paid by the due date set forth in this Contingency Placement Agreement, including but not necessarily Pennsylvania courts in the event of any disputes regarding this Agreement, and that this Agreement shall be governed by Pennsylvania.

9. **Termination of Agreement:** This Agreement may be terminated at any time at the option of the **Client** or by **SS** with thirty (30) days prior written notice of such termination. Notwithstanding the foregoing, no termination of the Agreement shall relieve **Client** of its obligation to pay compensation to SS in connection with any identified SS candidate referred prior to the termination of this Agreement. This Agreement supersedes all previous Placement Agreements between **SalesSource, Inc** and the **Client.**

Please sign and date this document to indicate **Client's** acceptance of the terms of the Agreement and return it to us as soon as possible, either by mail or by FAX.

Client's Authorized Signature

Print Name and Title _____

Company _____

Address _____

SalesSource Recruiting, Inc.
Authorized Signature _____

Diane O'Brien- Managing Director

Client Elevator Speech

Example:

Hi, I'm xxxxx, and wanted to introduce myself to you. I'm a recruiter in the (medical industry), and noticed you had an opening for a sales rep in NYC. I have someone I thought you might be interested in, and curious if I could shoot his resume over to you?

Obtain contact info, email. Ask pertinent questions:

"Do you work with many outside recruiters or agencies?"

"Do you ever retain one recruiting partner, or are you only contingency?

"If I send someone that looks to be a fit, should I send my contract terms over, or do you have your own to work from?"

"Please email back the contract, and thoughts on candidate. When's the best way to send you candidates for your other openings?

"Are there certain openings you could use help with right now?"

***Be sure to keep call brief, but get as much information as you can during this first call. See if you connect personally, and if so, speak to how you can add value to this person's time and job by finding them great people fast, and being easy to work with.

Invest time sending some good candidates, but don't go too far until you have a contract in place. Usually, you can use that first strong candidate to hook them into further negotiations. Plus, it's better to negotiate terms when there is someone they want to hire in the works. It gives you a little more leverage than if you were agreeing to standard terms with no one in play.

Job Oder Example (1):

Date:

Company:

Job:

Package:

Why Open:

Territory:

Key Cities to live:

Blurb:

Manager:
Manager's Hot buttons:

Candidate Profile:

Buzz words to search from:

Competitive Companies to source from:

Websites:
Training Date:

Job Order Example (2):

Job Order

Date: 11/8/06

Company: xxxxx Solutions

Job: Selling subscription service applications for PACS
Package: 70-80K base/ 150K Oppty

Why Open:

Territory: 1.Texas
　　　　　　2.New England

Key Cities to live: 1.Houston
　　　　　　　　　　　2. NJ/NY

Blurb: Hi there,

I have a job opportunity in your area that I think you may be interested in. It's representing an industry leader in the teleradiology market.

This is a six figure, first year opportunity with a nice base package.

If interested in hearing more, pls forward your resume in word format to (insert email), and I'll be in touch to discuss further.

Also, if you are not in the market, but know anyone else who may be a good fit-I offer $1K finder fees upon placement-

Look forward to talking soon,

Manager: Arman xxxxx

Manager's Hot buttons:

Candidate Profile: Must have experience with PACS/ teleradiology/ service sales

Buzz words to search from: teleradiology, information technology, service sales, PACS, more to come......

Competitive Companies to source from: Ikon Medical, Sedera, Voxar, Dynamic Imaging, Merge, more to come.......

Job Order Example:

Websites: xxxxx.com

Placement Fee: $18,000.00						
	Job Order					
Contact:	Recruiting Manager: Diane O'Brien					
	P:610-935-4858/F:610-935-4857					
	dobrien@fusionsalespartners.com					
Date:	10/11/2002					
Target Hire Date:	11/15/2002					
Company/ Position:	Agilent - Sales Manager	(2 positions: East & West coast)				
Job Description:						
	Lead and manage a sales team in the development of business within large enterprises (Fortune 1000) and Federal government. Rapidly build a team of "A" players while executing a strategic selling plan and managing the existing MR Network.					
Job Requirements:						
Must Have:						
	Must have a bachelors degree from an accredited college.					
	Minimum 2-3 years successful experience (ranked in top 20%) as a sales manager leading a technical products sales force.					
	Minimum 3-5 years successful experience (ranked in top 20%) as a sales representative.					
	Experience in sales/sales management with products/services that address IT Network Trouble Shooting/IT Management/ Network Diagnostic Solutions.					
	Passionate about selling and sales leadership.					
	Must have the finesse to be able to build a Partnership with key contacts in Agilent.					
	Must be a "Leader", not a "Manager".					
	Expertise selling to the large enterprise (Forutune1000) and Federal Government.					
	Intelligent, quick & autonomous- this is a new market with huge growth potential- sales manager must be able to rapidly "crack the code" with his/her team.					
Highly Desired:						
Territory:	East Coast/ West Coast		**Overnight Travel Required:**		Yes	
Compensation:	Guarantee of $120K paid monthly.					
	Realistic 1st year with incentives $150,000 - $175,000.					
	Benefits: Eligible to participate in Fusion's Health Insurance (Care First/BCBS), Dental (MetLife), Vision, Group Life, Long Term Disability, 401(k) plan and 15 days free time off, as well as a paid holiday schedule.					
Company Info:	www.fusionsalespartners.com		**Career Path:**			
	www.agilent.com					
Product Info:	General Info: www.onenetworks.com		**Competitors:** www.networkassociates.com			
	Cost Of Product:		www.fluke.com			
	Average Sale: $30-50K					
	Sales Cycle: 2-6 months					
Comments:	Will be the first of two sales managers in this segment.					
	Inheriting book of business ($12 million nationally) with active pipe line.					
	Will manage 10-12 reps.					

Chapter 3

Week 3: The Candidates & Resumes

Candidates

This chapter is going to read very similar to Chapter 2 on Clients, however, now we are going to focus on the Candidate side. We'll assume you have the job and the contract, so now you will need to find the candidates. You will utilize the same methodology of asking yourself the right questions as to who, what, when, where, and how, when figuring these questions out.

On the candidate side, who will be your ideal candidate? This will be determined by reviewing the job order and job description, to come up with a profile of your ideal candidate. This profile will be something you can type up in a brief paragraph, and also practiced to say in an 'elevator speech' if you had to tell someone else what exactly you're looking for. Remember, whether in recruiting or life, you never get to the right answers, without asking the right questions. So, we need to ask ourselves, who are we looking for? Where will we find them? How will we find them? Then what? This is where the resumes will take front and center stage. The client may just bring one job order with them, but when searching for candidates, you'll have to screen tons of resumes. You'll be talking to a lot of frogs til you meet your prince. Again, hope you enjoy people.

When we start making the calls, if you don't like talking to new people every day, and are feeling more and more uncomfortable, think twice about recruiting. If you like it, regardless of how scary it may feel to be doing something new, that's a good sign. If you start having good conversations that seem to be energizing you thru your day, making the bad phone calls tolerable, you're on the right path. When time is flying by, and you're having fun, you're on to something good for you. So remember those feelings when they happen, because you'll have to recall those, just like your mentor, when going thru yucky days. So, now onto finding the Candidates!

Where to find candidates? Where's the Source?

Where does the Headhunting Housewife find great candidates after she's found her first Client? You're going to find your candidates in many ways. You will utilize the large job board sites such as Monster, CareerBuilder, Indeed, and others. You will utilize career directories like Zoom info, Capital IQ, Hoovers, and others. You will use networking sites such as LinkedIn and Facebook, among others. LinkedIn has changed the world of recruiting, as it's a great way to database your clients and candidates, as well as utilizing it for searching.

You will also do some good old fashion headhunting by calling good people in the market you are searching to ask for good people. After years of recruiting you will build your own personal database that makes this job simpler, but until then, you are lucky to live in an era where people are putting most of their professional information on the worldwide web. You can google certain jobs and find candidates that could be helpful thru press releases or their own buzz words that get pulled from their profiles on various networking sites.

It will feel like you are looking for that needle in the haystack. But as you utilize your different resources, and follow the trail from one person's referral to another, you often end up with a handful of people that are going to fit your client's job order. Be sure to learn all the advanced tips needed to do the advanced searches on candidates, or else you could be wasting a lot of time. If you are learning to do this on your own at home, the way that I first started, you won't have the benefit to learn the easy way by simply watching someone in the office perform the same task. If you could get a couple years inside a recruiting office, it makes it so much easier to start to learn from watching, instead of figuring it out yourself. However, there's something to be said for figuring it out on your own as well.

Be sure to take advantage of all free training. Monster will show you how to use the Boolean tips and how to perform advanced searches. You'll learn quickly what works for you, and how to save your searches so you're not duplicating efforts. You can also get free training on LinkedIn from them, or from free webinars hosted by people who are experts in the field. Take advantage of all of these free tutorials, as it will save you loads of time if you're trying to figure out what is worth your time and money.

We've covered where you are going to go to find them, but you still need to figure out how to get them. Similar to the client side, you'll need a clear understanding of who you are looking for. This will be a profile that you will write up based upon your job description from the client calls. From your profile, you will know who you want to target as your searching thru the hundreds of profiles and resumes. And also like we did on the Client side, you will need a new elevator speech which will give a two minute run down to your potential candidate of what this job you are calling about entails? This two minute speel can be left on their voicemail if you don't catch them live, but ideally you want to get a 20 minute first phone conversation which peaks their interest in the job, and to see if they are a possible fit?

From here you will follow up with an email detailing more company information, and requesting an updated copy of their resume. After which time, you will follow up with a phone interview to learn more about them as a viable candidate. There are many more details to cover when finding and landing the right candidate, but for now I hope this gives you a broad understanding of how Headhunters from home, or in Corporate offices, find their candidates.

What are you looking for in a Candidate?

As mentioned, you'll want to develop a Candidate Profile based off of your Job description to stay on target. Before you make your first phone call, be sure to develop a one page profile of exactly what you are seeking. This should come right off the job description and job order you obtained from the client call, adding any details that you picked up during phone conversations with the hiring manager.

I'll give an example of this at the end of this chapter. This Candidate Profile will keep you clear on exactly what you're looking for, and you'll use it as a quick reference, while tweaking and fine tuning it along the way.

How to Get Qualified Candidates?

The how to get candidates comes into play by utilizing your resume screening tactics covered from the free seminars you'll get from the job boards as discussed. They will show you how to do the searches to find the best fitting group of qualified candidates. From here, you'll want to learn how to scan resumes quickly for exactly what you're looking for. You'll be reviewing dates, how long they were at a job, if there are any gaps in resumes, and a checklist of other items that correspond to your job description and candidate profile. I've included a resume checklist at the end of the chapter as well for a more detailed example.

After gathering the qualified resumes, you'll then utilize your "elevator speech" when you start making the calls. You'll be leaving lots of messages in the beginning, but your phone will start to ring a lot after the first couple days of you putting calls out there. You want to be careful to quickly engage the candidate with a quick sentence about the opportunity, but be sure you have them somewhat "hooked" and interested before turning the call into a fact finding mission for yourself. You'll want to utilize the checklist, and job specific questions to review their background and get a sense of the kind of person you have on the other end of the phone. This will take some practice, and the more you do it, the better you'll get. Be sure to watch the clock, so you don't run too long, as these are just preliminary screens. You don't want to invest too much time until you know you have someone the client would like to take a deeper look at. Your goal is to be fast and effective in finding a handful of people that fit the bill, and that you feel could potentially be the right person for the job.

It's also a good idea to leave the first phone call with giving them a little homework to do, such as researching the client and job opportunity further. This is easily done by getting their personal email so you can send them some links and a little more info. This is also a good way to really see how much interest they have after you hang up the phone. Wait a couple days to see if they follow-up with you. You don't want to have to chase and convince someone of a good opportunity. Once you've had your time with them, let it sit, and see if it's meant to be. They'll call back if so. If not, move on. On occasion you may have someone very good that needs a little more convincing, but if you still feel like you have to "sell" them on the job by the 3rd conversation, this person may be wasting time, only to turn down the job at the very end. The right person will be eager and interested to learn more, without you having to put in too much work. Remember, you're offering a better role for them with better money, and you're just a piece of the puzzle in helping them realize the opportunity. The old adage you can bring a horse to water comes to mind....you can't make them drink. So, be sure to do your best, but then let life do what it's supposed to do...no need to force it.

Marketing your candidate

Much of the success you will have is established in your little routines each day. The quick email you shoot the manager on your candidate, the phone call to describe the role, the touch points to get temperature checks at every turn. When marketing your candidate, the details are again so important and what can make or break you. Remember to review the Recruiting Process, realizing that like anything, recruiting is a series of steps, from start to finish. Anyone with enough drive and sense could be a recruiter, and many try. But what makes the difference will be your salesmanship at every turn. It will be your constant awareness of the system, and how to improve this recruiting machine, so that you can become more efficient and more successful as the years go by. When you're on the phone "selling" the Hiring Manager on a candidate, or when you're selling the candidate on the job- it will be those brief conversations that will decide if you close the deal. And when I mention the word, selling, I hope you don't take that the wrong way. Many people who don't have a marketing or sales background still associate sales people with the typical used car salesman. Someone trying to sell you something you don't need, or upgrade you to stuff you don't need, to make a profit, at your expense. However, I'm talking about good salesmanship. Positive selling where you really are looking out for your client's best interest, as well as your candidate's. In the recruiting world, because you are dealing in moving people from job to job, I feel that you have an extra level of social responsibility than many other jobs. And to be a good sales person, one who cares about the relationships, more than the transaction, is critical.

Recruiting is a Science and an Art. The Science is in understanding the process and plan, but the casual conversations and scheduling details are the Art of Recruiting, and are often more important than any mechanics.

Selling and Coaching

Setting the stage for a positive meeting is so important. Same with setting the stage for the first phone call, or coaching the candidate on the manager's "hot buttons." How do you know the manager's hot buttons? Because the last candidate filled you in on them after his interview when you probed about the questions he was asked, or perhaps you uncovered some on your first call with the manager. And similar to not taking the "selling" word in the wrong manner, be careful not to take the "coaching" word in the wrong light as well.

I've gotten into many conversations with other recruiters, as well as hiring managers and clients on this topic. I view it as part of your role as a good recruiter to help coach and mentor your candidate into the right position for them. I would never recommend coaching them the "right" answers, or trying to give them inside information which would just put a "square peg in a round hole" anyway. However, good coaching is very useful. To speak to your candidate the night before a big interview to review key points, or ask for last minute concerns, or remind them of who their audience will be and what they know about them so far is crucial.

You don't want your candidate to go into an interview with one resume in hand expecting to meet his future boss, and end up having a panel of people in a board room. Helping your candidate know what to expect is just as important as setting your clients up in the right manner. Both parties need to be 'debriefed' and 'coached' to a certain extent to help make this process run smoothly and get to a clean finish.

I'm driving this point home once again, because to simply follow the steps will not make you successful, and now that we've come to a point where you're ready to put your candidate in front of the Hiring Manager for the first time...well, this is not a time to let things ride! This is where you remember how important your role is in this process. You are the quarterback of this whole deal, so you need to run the ball home. That's why good recruiters get paid well-not everyone can read these little details in people, and know how to smoothly get to the end game.

Review the checklist with the candidate, see attached. Are they prepared for the interview, did they do additional research, review the companies job description of this role? Do they have extra copies of the resume ready in case there are multiple interviewers? Have you confirmed the correct phone numbers and addresses of the meeting in case someone gets delayed or changes need to be made last minute.

Are they 'dressing for success'? Do they understand this isn't the time to negotiate money? Do they have questions ready for the client when it's their turn to ask questions?

Would a business plan or 30-60-90 day plan help cinch the deal if they really want this job? You could send a template. And don't forget the important question of how do they feel about the job? Are there any concerns being expressed at this point? The concerns are something you can help bring to the Hiring Managers attention when appropriate and while prepping him, and will come in handy when you explain that they must also sell the candidate on the job if they in fact want that person.

An invaluable question before the meeting is, if you were offered the job after your meeting, would you take it? You'll be surprised at the answers you get to this one. And this is just as important to ask on the other side to the Hiring Manager. Are you prepared to make an offer to this candidate if she's the one?

Other important questions to candidates would be what kind of compensation would they be leaving on the table if they were offered the job. Finding these things out now, and not later, is crucial. Have they talked to their spouse about the job- how does their wife or husband feel about it?

When advising young recruiters, many are so surprised by how personal my questions get, but I don't think I've ever offended anyone. Well, maybe, especially when hiring in more conservative parts of the country. Luckily for me, living in the Mid-Atlantic region near NYC, everyone is pretty direct. Learning the nuances of the different regions of our country does get interesting. I can speak to that more later!

It's a good idea to ask certain questions more than once during the process, since things change. For example, if the manager on your first call together needed someone asap, and was ready to hire the right person as soon as you found them, but suddenly changes their tune when presented with the right person- you'll have more investigating to do.

There are numerous scenarios that may be the reason for delays, which could include headcount issues, territory changes, budgeting problems, and other, but we'll cover that later. The point we want to convey at this time, is to continue asking the important questions to both your candidate and clients. I've had territories change over-night, or a company- wide policy change in the midst of the process, so often it may seem like a mystery why that LA opening that was so hot, is now moving so slow, but this is all part of the game, and you have to keep "temperature checking." Although you may have spent numerous phone calls with both parties, they have not. Do not forget to highlight the key points on selling both sides, and to do so thru both methods of phone calls, and emails.

When marketing the candidate before the "send out" or face to face, I would always advise to cover both. I would often use email for the quick factual hits....top 10% producer, rookie of the year, presidents club member...the quick bullets that show the candidate in strong light. But then I would use the phone call, which is much more personal to express the enthusiasm I have for the candidate- you can only get this thru voice, no matter how strong a writer you may be. And you cannot uncover any concerns thru email- it's just too much to write. Marketing the candidate this way, thru both the phone and email is again, nothing mind blowing. But, having the clear intention behind each email and phone call, and maintaining that discipline thru your career can be tougher than it sounds.

Effective Phone Conversations

Alright, so back to the phone and emails. You are calling candidates, tracking down leads, making notes on good resumes, leaving lots of messages. You'll find a funny pattern emerge, as for those first couple of days with a new job order, you are putting tons of calls out, but no one's calling back....you may tend to get worried. And then by day three or so, your phone is lighting up, and you can't keep up. This is where your organizational skills will be key, and keeping track of everyone in your database with good notes will be important. You'll have a form of short hand you'll utilize- starring good resumes. Scoring the phone calls from 1-10. Placing little flags next to things of concern. Many more details that you'll do in a couple second scan of a resume, or sizing someone up quickly on the phone.

You may also see a pattern emerge with good candidates, that the one's you star or like the best may be the same ones not getting back to you. You have to remember that the good ones are usually pretty happy and not actively looking. These are the passive candidates that you want. They may not call you back, and you may have to chase them down. A previous consulting job I took, was only after they called me several times. I already had a good gig for another firm, and wasn't looking to take on any more work, but when the recruiter basically left me a message asking for a quick phone call with the CEO, I took the call. What girl doesn't liked to be chased anyway, and although I wasn't playing hard to get- I would be hard to get since I was happy enough. But then again, to finish the story, what is happy enough- if there's another level of happiness, I'm open to listen. And yes, sometimes the grass is much greener! Not always, and I did months of homework to make sure it would be, but taking those calls put the pool in my backyard, so never be close minded.

I give these examples not to brag about my experiences, but to provide real life examples of persistence, and why it's good to be open to new opportunities. And also as a reminder to not judge someone for not returning a call....in fact, taking judgment off the table is a good idea all together. Granted, you'll be making judgment calls on someone's abilities all the time, but I'm talking about leaving the negative judgments or things you may take personal off the table, like someone not calling you back.

So, back to the process. After days of sending emails, if the 'starred' candidates did not reach out to me with a copy of their resume, I would call them. At least the email sent first would give them a chance to review my email, along with some job details, and look forward to talking. Another 'warm call' instead of cold call, just like we learned in getting this job order. Same idea applies to getting the candidate.

The other thing I would often do in the first few days of searching is leave my office number off of the email, so I wouldn't get inundated with calls, while I was in my precious sourcing time- that first week. Even with many of the job boards, like Monster, that show the persons recent resume in word format- many may be older versions, and by the time you're a couple days into searching- when receive an email back with the attached resume, and look at it a second time- it may not be as good, now that you've found better ones in more recent searches. So, again, although on this first search, for sheer practice of doing phone calls, and feeling like a recruiter- you may want your phone to be ringing. But just remember, you'll want to eventually fall into a nice pattern, where you control your day- not the phone or other people.

Maintain Weekly Schedule

Let's say it's Wednesday, you did 3 hours on Monday, 3 Tuesday, 2 more Wednesday morning, started putting calls out by Wednesday afternoon. And if you've done your job well early on, the energy you have put out will now start returning to you. The phone will be ringing. Your once solace time of 3 hour increments searching is now eaten up by three phone calls, and some follow up stuff. Out of the three people you spoke to- none seem to be a fit- one just took a job, the other's resume looked great, but was awful on the phone- low energy and negative, with a couple layoffs to boot, and the third wanted more money to make a move. This is where your search continues, but you're leaving the phones open to take incoming calls.

Emails are going out. You're putting some calls out to the great ones, you're data basing as you go, and speaking to candidates when they call back, trying to keep your preliminary phone calls to under ½ hour. You'll find the good ones end up being fun to speak to, at least in my line of recruiting- sales people- and those are often the ones that get the job- you actually enjoyed the conversation and they seem perfect. You'll need 3-5 of those for the client to find the perfect one, but will cover that later as well.

It's Friday morning, wow- one week is down- the client is waiting. You may have a solid candidate, or you may still find yourself looking. Either way, you want to send an email just re-assuring your client that you've been screening thru multiple potentials, and want to be sure you don't waste his time. Often, if this is a new client- I remind him that the first one or two may not be a match- but that's typically how you get closer to his ideal candidate- by getting his feedback on what he liked or didn't- often items that are never spoken about on the first phone call or on any job description. His biases and hot buttons will come out during the first few candidates you send, and you will start to get a better understanding of exactly who he is looking for. It never ceased to amaze me after the hundreds of jobs I've searched on, and the numerous Hiring Managers I've worked with, that they don't realize the level of detail the search entails. I mean there is a bit of matchmaking involved.

One of the questions you remember asking on your first meeting is where the manager came from prior to that company. Reason being is that you'll find out they will also have a soft spot in many instances for someone similar to them. Many books claim that the manager wants to hire someone just like him or her, and that is partially true. The better manager will understand that tendency and be open to a diverse group- but it's definitely good to understand this mentality when working with your Hiring Manager.

To get back to it being Friday and you want to touch base with the client. Let's say you have found someone you think could be a match. There are different schools of thought here. I remember coming to the conclusion a few months into being a recruiter- that the first great person I found that was what I thought to be, a hole in one, never seemed to get the job. I started holding off on sending my best candidate as the first one- instead sending maybe my second favorite to be the guinea pig. A recruiter friend with more experience confirmed that yes, you never want to send your best person first- I think I'm quoting my good friend and mentor, Dave

Kline here....I believe he said to think of it like real estate. You just started your search for a home, you're excited to find your perfect house, and the agent takes you to the first one...how often does that person say yes, this is the one, I want to buy? I'm guessing rarely. They may buy it after shopping around to look at 10 more houses, and then end up coming back to their original.

Problem being with that scenario, that people, like houses, do not stay on the market long. And unlike houses, good candidates that don't get strong buying signals from the manager early, usually lose interest as well. So- I have been known to hold back my best for the 2nd or 3rd submittal. But what I also learned is that these techniques are so subjective based on the Hiring Manager you work with. I have had clients that didn't mess around, and especially after working with me for many years- knew that I did a thorough job of screening, and I would be able to send that first one and they would hire that first one. I suppose I would re-cant getting burnt on new clients, and often try to strategize a bit more on the order I sent- but you'll have to be careful and figure this out depending on your client and your relationship.

So, let's say you decide to send the quick email. Keep emails short, so your clients will actually read it.

You have many candidates you're still screening thru, attached is one that you like- you bullet or write a few sentences on what makes them a fit-

- Top 10% of their Baltimore sales team selling x-ray equipment.

- Put herself thru school, true hunter sales person-
- Territory and money good fit, and would like to learn more on this opportunity.

May I schedule you a phone interview? She's available Tuesday at 9am or Wednesday at 11am?

Something to this effect. The client will either want to schedule, thinking the resume looks good, or they may want to speak to you to learn more first about the candidate before committing to a phone time in their busy schedule.

This is where it's very important to build client trust, and make it evident from your very first few calls, that you add value to them. You, in fact, save them time, by being the middle man, or woman, by screening out all the candidates that are not right for the job.

Although you do want to establish a rapport and good relationship with the client on every call- you also want to be aware that their time is valuable, and to keep your calls to a minimum. I've had recruiters I worked with when I was in the HR role that were very nice, and we may have had great 20 or 30 minute conversations, but unless they benefited the business in some way- I often wouldn't take their calls again unless they had a candidate I wanted to speak to.

Lesson I'm saying here is to keep it professional, keep it brief, letting them know they are busy, and just need about 15 minutes of their time to review a candidate or two, and go from there. So, to review your schedule and timetable- You got the job order Monday- you're sending your first candidate Friday- ahead of schedule. And you enjoy your weekend, preparing for another week of sourcing and screening next week. You'll repeat the job board sourcing increments, now mixed with screening candidates.

And regarding some strategy- do not send anyone else until you get feedback on the first, 'guinea pig' candidate. This is important- you don't want the client to think that good candidates are a dime a dozen, and you can just keep them coming. Your goal should be to only have to submit 3 candidates, 5 max in order to land a job. Now, that number could go up, if there's territory changes, or your person bails, and you have to start a search over. But for the most part, to up your odds of closing your job, source heavy the first week, screen heavy while continuing to source the second week. Follow up on loose ends the third week, and with any luck and determination- the baton should really be passing onto the client by week 2-3. This is where you can sit back and wait, while your candidate or candidates are taken thru the process with client.

They will typically need to pass a phone interview with HR, and/or the Hiring Mgr. Perhaps a phone call with the Managers boss. Then onto a personal interview- the live interview, or in some instances a video conference. From here, the chosen candidate is typically brought back for a final interview- always live, and meeting all decision makers, with the hope of leaving the interview with a verbal or written offer.

During this process, when your candidate or candidates are going thru these steps- You want to be quietly following up on both sides, making sure to let the other side know where there may be some points of contention. This is especially important if no HR is involved- but even then, you want to stay on top of the progress.

This is another 'fine line' in recruiting that I believe can separate the good from the great recruiters.

Resumes

When you're a recruiter, your life will become about reading and scanning resumes. In the beginning, you'll probably find yourself reading every line, and deciding who seems to be best to actually reach out to. But as time goes by, and you get better at learning what to look for, you'll really end up scanning resumes broadly versus reading every little detail. It's really the details that are between the lines in the empty space that ends up meaning more.

For example, are there any gaps in the resumes? Is there an evident progression of success from one job to another? Any layoffs that maybe are not mentioned, or are they unemployed right now? The resumes may not have any of this information written, but you will learn to read between the lines to find this out, without ever having to waste time on a phone call. Now, when I say 'waste' time, keep in mind no one should be considered a waste of time. And almost every call gains you some insight into where you need to go next, however, you could spend all your hours of your day speaking to the wrong people and asking the wrong questions. So, to be effective, and the best recruiter you can be for both you and the candidate, you need to learn to ask the right questions, and focus on the important things. I'll attach my **First Phone Interview Checklist** as an example of some things to look for and ask about. The obvious ones being the date of college, first job thru last job, checking dates have months by them too, so not to miss any gap between jobs. How the resume over all looks- is it professional? Or have more typos and formatting mistakes then it needed to? I was more tolerant of most on a typo here or there, or a misspelled word. When I learned to spot a diamond in the rough, I never minded running my own spellcheck to clean someone's resume up...especially when I saw good people get hired, that didn't necessarily have the best resumes. You'll see this for yourself as well. You'll also notice I gave a lot of weight to the other things you pull off a phone interview that you can't get by reading someone on paper. Energy level, confidence, tone of voice, fast talker, slow talker, forever go on and on and on talker. Happy, Sad? Do they sound like they are drunk or smoke a pack a day, or are the clear and concise, answering your questions directly and professionally.

How are they conversationally? Easy to talk to, or making you uncomfortable? I'm sure you're lists of what to look for off of the resume will evolve and become your own. Since my focus was typically from sales reps to marketing directors to managers and others with "sales skills," I often looked for the same qualities. Obviously, when hiring a CEO, I may look more for someone with creativity, and vision. Someone who is an obvious good leader, and inspirational to speak to. If looking for an engineer, your list would be different. But I think you get what I'm saying. It's going to be 50% art...finding out who this person really is quickly, and 50% science....in finding out if the resume matches the qualifications, and dates, numbers, and timing match up. And after you've done all you can do, you still have to leave the rest to the 'chemistry and culture' fit that your candidate has with the hiring manager, and that is very subjective as well.

More on Job Boards when searching Resumes

It's important to remember that when searching Monster, LinkedIn, Zoom Info, Capital IQ, or any other database, that you want your system to be fast and effective. For example if I wanted to spend my morning on Monster, I would log on, do the search, save the search, and plan on spending the next 2-3 hours uninterrupted of scanning and reviewing resumes. I would use their methods of saving resumes, as well as my own, of emailing the resume to my own inbox for saving in my database. I would still print out the very strong resumes, but usually would not call anyone during this time slot. I would email. I'd have a standard email blurb that I made up and saved as a signature, so I could quickly email anyone I liked. It would be a simple hello, who I was, and I had a job opportunity that they may be interested in. I would give something to entice them, like the salary range, or company it was for, and leave my contact info. I think I mentioned before that sometimes I would also request their resume without leaving my number, so my phone wouldn't be ringing off the hook just yet. That way, I was getting feelers put out while on Monster, but not getting bogged down in calls or other stuff. Later, as I reviewed all the candidates I liked, I would follow up with my contact info or phone calls to the really good ones. Many people won't send their resume blindly. Many will though. You'll have to see what works best for you.

Although I'm giving you how I did it, keep in mind that thru out this journey, you are just utilizing my experience and example as one way.

Hopefully, it will help you when you find yourself falling into a pattern, to know it may be similar to a pattern hundreds of other at-home- Mom's and other at-home-headhunters fell into. When you know you're not alone, or someone else did the same thing, or similar, it can help validate that you are on the right path, and helps you to stay motivated. That's what I'm hoping these stories and examples do for you. And if you're able to follow almost directly by example- that can just be icing on the cake for you, as you don't have to develop all this stuff from scratch, or by learning the 'hard way.'

Posting Jobs

I had never been a big fan of posting jobs. Except lately, in seeing how LinkedIn has evolved, that is one site I can see posting on. However, when I use to post positions, which was very rare, I quickly realized to open a new generic email address because your email box will become filled with junk. Or set up your outlook, so it automatically deposits into a file that you can review on your own time.

The reason I was never a fan of posting jobs was because I ended up spending so much time going thru so many junk emails and resumes. And then the candidates would be calling or emailing checking what the status was. It was a great way to become really, really busy, and very, very ineffective. I have always preferred to quietly, scan the resumes, and get references from calls I made to good people, and have myself being the one to make the call to someone who looked good. And I typically would not spend any time on the phone until I got that resume.

Again, with Linked In and Facebook these days, you can now find someone's background without waiting for you to send a resume, but it's still a good idea. Not only does it give you more control over process, but it also lets you see who follows up properly to forward you a resume upon your request. You can get a sense of the interest level before you ever make a call. This leads very well into our next segment on making that first 'cold call.' If you take the write steps with emails and some correspondence via email first, the first phone conversation is not so cold. It's more of a warm call.

Warm- Calls to the Candidate

We've covered the basics of the first interview, but remember the first conversation doesn't typically jump into a full interview. Usually, you'll perform a 20 min call first to make sure the interest is there, sell the job, and give them some homework to do some more research on the company. This helps sift out the ones that won't be a fit anyway. When you schedule a more in depth phone interview, that's where you'll use the phone interview checklist.

Later, you'll do a full interview in person, and then a Final. I'll give you templates of those as well, although I'm sure you'll need to customize your own. Although you may never have had the luxury of working in a recruiting office before becoming a recruiter, it was a nice benefit later in my career to work alongside other recruiting companies and see how they did things. Surprisingly, although I had to figure it out on my own early on, they were all basically doing the same steps, but just customizing it a bit based on their market and business models. But the steps in recruiting, along with time tables, and process were all pretty much the same.

When sitting with a CEO, and watching him recruit other CEO's for companies, it was enlightening to see the same questions being asked, but I also gained new insight in what worked specifically for him. There was another CEO client (later a mentor), I worked with that took me to a meeting with Christian & Timbers where I also got to watch firsthand how different recruiters do their jobs. Before, for all the jobs, it was just myself, and later, sometimes sitting with managers that were doing final interviews on candidates I already pre-selected. But listening to other CEO's use their recruiting and business development skills, made me realize how much I could have learned from these type of mentors earlier in my career. I ended up doing fine on my own, but if I could have listened to someone of their caliber, when I was starting my business, I'm sure I would have been placing a lot more higher end and C-Level positions earlier in my career. Once again, recognizing that the questions and the process were so similar, was validating, but also watching how to control the call, and how to handle every call with the same template in mind was useful. Most executives didn't have a script or template, as I had created for myself, and other managers thru the years, but most were basically asking the same questions. Peter Groop and Andy Towne, two CEO's that had a great influence on me, continue to be some of the best recruiters and CEO's I ever worked with, and I owe them lots of gratitude for taking me under their wing, and helping me become a better recruiter, business developer, and ultimately an entrepreneur.

My main point being that if you ever have the opportunity to work in a recruiting office to learn these skills, that's a bonus. But considering a lot of you are specifically looking at this career choice, so you don't have to go to an office, I'm here to re-assure you that it's not necessary. Plus, offices have lots of people and overhead, and again, your placement fee would be cut multiple ways. At times in your career, when learning something new, or striking out in a different direction, it makes sense to take a smaller cut, but keep in mind, that the one making the rules is usually making the money, so start out feeling like your own boss, so you can be that ideally.

I'm currently consulting again and splitting the profits more, so I'm not stuck at my desk so much on the phone (there would be no time to write!). But like I said, there will be a time and place for being a part in a larger puzzle, or then again, later moving on in creating the puzzle.

Working at a desk in your own home office can be heaven for many years. Or it can later become confining. Wherever this career takes you, it's nice to know recruiting can offer stay at home time, or going to an office time, or traveling around country time. You can custom tailor your career within recruiting as you better understand the different facets of it, and how to best utilize your unique skill sets.

Choose to "Headhunt from Home," as you are learning now, or take this knowledge to land a recruiting role in an office one day, aka "Headhunting in Heels"....or some perfect combo that works for you now and in the future!

Week 3 Checklist:

Week 3- Find Candidates

- ✓ Review Job Board tips, Monster, Career Builder
- ✓ Learn how to post on other boards; craigslist, networking sites, etc
- ✓ Learn how to mass email candidates
- ✓ Learn how to efficiently save resumes/notes for database
- ✓ Maintain weekly schedule of cold calling/emailing for candidates
- ✓ Develop email template for candidate sourcing
- ✓ Learn the art of speed reading Resumes

Attachments:

Profile

Resume checklists from Phone Interview Templates

Email "Blurb" Examples

Phone Interview 1

Phone Interview 2

Face to Face Interview

Final Interview

Profile Example:

(Based off of job order, job description, and things you learned on your phone conversation with client. Include Hiring Manager's soft spots or hot buttons)

Candidate Profile for GE Mammography Search

Manager: Betty- Regional Sales Mgr- Women's Healthcare
Manager's Hot buttons: Betty- likes copier reps, telesales background

Candidate Profile: Typical company profile, young, hungry, capital experience, top 10%, hard sales numbers

Buzz words to search from: copier sales, mammography, Source One, Instrumentarium, Quantum, ADP, Xerox, AT&T, MCI, women's healthcare, breast imaging, capital equipment, medical device sales

Competitive Companies to source from: Instrumentarium..

Email "Blurb" Examples:

If you are interested in hearing more, please forward your resume in Word format to "email address" and I will be in touch to discuss further.

Also, if you are not on the job market, but know other good reps-I offer up to $1K finder fees upon placement.

Hi there,

I saw your resume on a job board, and think you may be interested in a medical sales position I have in your area. It's a six figure job oppty representing Kodak selling X-ray film and equipment to hospitals in the Omaha market.

If you're interested in hearing more, pls email me a word format of your resume to *diane@salessourceinc.com* and call me at 610-935-4858 to discuss further.

Also, if you are no longer in the job market, but know someone that may be a good fit- I offer $1K finder fees if I make the placement.

Look forward to speaking,

Diane O'Brien

SalesSource

610-935-4858

Hi There,

I have a job opportunity in your area representing an industry leader in Women's Healthcare Imaging. This is a six figure first year position...look forward to speaking with you soon.

Recruiter's Elevator Speech to Candidate (1st call)

<u>Recruiter's Pre-Screen Phone</u>

Do you have a few minutes?

Okay, great...Let me just give you a quick run-down of the job opportunity, and if it sounds interesting enough- I'll get into further detail...

Hook:

This position is representing Sonosite.... have you ever heard of them? Well, it's a great company- they are the industry leader in hand held ultrasound (portable ultrasounds) market. They are partnering with another company named Market-Bridge, to hire a sales team to focus on the physician market place... Sonosite already owns the market in the hospitals, but are looking to grow the physician based business.

It will be a specialized sales force dedicated to that market- ob/gyns, vascular surgeons, etc.

These are great opportunities- it's a six figure first year job- you'll be able to make about $150K first year. Salaried position, highly commission based, full benefits, car allowance, 401k, etc.

Temp Check: Before I get too much deeper, so far....does this sound like it could be a fit for you?

Yes- Great, let me find out a few things about you to make sure you're a good fit for this position as well- go onto pre-screen...

No-   Well, I'm new as a recruiter- I'd like to get you to my manager who get better answer some of those questions for you-
But what I can tell you, is that we (SalesSource) only hire six figure a year sales positions in the high end, medical capital equipment. Typically we only hire for the industry leaders like SonoSite, GE, Hologic, Siemens, etc... these are very realistic, high paying sales jobs- would love to be able to forward you onto to Diane, my manager, who works with the client directly... Is it okay if just ask you some preliminary questions to make sure that you qualify for the job, like the territory??

Pre-Screen/Qualify:
1-As far as t**he territory**....it covers..... Is that a fit for you?   Do you currently cover that area now?
2-What have you been earning the past few years, **W-2**, wise?
Great- you're right in line with the profile they look for- earning $80-120K, but probably itching to break six figures, or earn more- like this $150K spot.
Have you ever worked straight commission before?
3-So, are you currently looking to **leave your company?**
Why?
Close call:

Another Initial Phone Call Example:

Pre-Screen Information:
Leaving a Message

Hi, This is "Your Name" it's "Date/Time of Call (Eastern Time)". I'm a recruiter with SalesSource. You were referred to me as a strong salesperson in the "City" area and I currently have a job opportunity there that I think you may be interested in. It's selling capital imaging equipment, for an industry leader, a six figure a year job.

If you are interested in hearing more, Please give a call back to "Number (2x, slow and repeat your name)".

Also if you are not in the market...good people know good people, I offer $1K finder fees upon placement, so look forward to speaking with you either way!

Thanks-

Prescreen Phone Conversation

Hi, This is "Your Name" I'm a recruiter from SalesSource Inc. and I have a job opportunity you may be interested in. You were referred to me as a strong salesperson in your area.

Do you have a few minutes to talk?

Great, Let me give you a quick run-down of the job opportunity, and if it sounds interesting enough I will get into further detail....

HOOK:

This position is representing *Sonosite*.... Have you ever heard of them? Well, it's a great company. They are the industry leader in the hand held ultrasound market (portable ultrasound) They are partnering with another company named Market-Bridge, to hire a sales team to focus on the physician market place. Sonosite already owns the market in the hospitals, but are looking to grow the physician based business.

It will be a specialized sales force dedicated to the market of ob/gyns, vascular surgeons...

These are great opportunities- it's a six figure first year job- you'll be able to make about $150K first year. Salaried position, highly commission based, full benefits, car allowance, 401K.

TEMP CHECK:

Before I get too much deeper, so far....Does this sound like it could be a fit for you?

Yes- Great, let me find out a few things about you to make sure you're a good fit for this position as well.

No-Well, I'm new as a recruiter and I'd like to get you to my manager who could better answer some of those questions for you.

But what I can tell you, is that we (SalesSource) only hire six figure a year sales positions, in the high end, medical capital equipment....Typically we only hire for the industry leaders like SonoSite, GE, Hologic, Siemens....These are very realistic, high paying sales jobs.

I would love to be able to forward you onto Diane, my manager, who works with the client directly...Is it okay if I just ask you some preliminary questions to make sure that you qualify for the job, like the territory, for example?

Prescreen/ Qualify

1. As far as territory..... (Tell the area it covers)...Is it a fit for you? Do you currently cover that area now?
2. What have you been earning W-2 wise? Great you're right in line with the profile they look for-earning $80-120K, but probably itching to break six figures, or even more-like this $150K spot.
3. So, are you currently looking to leave your company? Why?

Thank them for time, and get their availability for the next few days for a phone screen with me. Also, if not on resume- get email and cell phone- and forward them a follow up email thanking them again, and giving them websites to review before the call with me.

*** Be sure to jot the above notes on the resume, and follow up with an email covering the above items, as well as any other thoughts from call (characteristics of candidate- energy level, kind, funny, excited about job, skeptical about job, etc..-see list of scorable traits)

***In email, have candidate name- city- Company in the Subject.
Need word in subject to know they have been screened vs. resume only?

Ex: Prescreened candidate- Mary X- Boston- MB/Sonosite

Recruiter Phone Interview Checklist Example:

Applicant Name: ☐☐☐☐☐

Date:

Gender of Applicant: Select One

Company/Position: ☐☐☐☐☐

Location: ☐☐☐☐☐

Screener's Phone Interview

Recommendation:

Yes   Applicant meets all requirements as specified on the Job Order

No   Applicant has not met all requirements, yet is qualified to continue in the interview process for the following reasons:

Comments: ☐☐☐☐☐

Income History

Past 3 years W2's: ☐☐☐☐☐   Previously Worked on Commission Only?
Select One

Income Level Desired: $☐☐☐☐☐

Interview Ratings

5=Excellent Match, 4=Great Match, 3=Good Match, 2=Acceptable, 1=Unacceptable

Select One

Select One First Impression
Select One Logical Career Path
Select One Energy Level/Enthusiasm
Select One Answers Questions Directly
Select One Well-Spoken
Select One Asks Strong Qualifying Questions
Select One Confidence Level
Select One Overall Phone Presence
Select One Integrity/Honesty
Select One Computer Proficiency

Select One Culture Match (Independent, Entrepreneurial)

Select One Positive Attitude

Select One Friendliness

Select One Team Player

Select One Industry Knowledge

Select One Other: ☐☐☐☐☐

Comments: ☐☐☐☐☐

Checklist Questions

Are there any unusual gaps in resume? Why?

Confirm College Degree

Reason for Leaving Current Company

Currently Employed?

Territory Coverage

Strong Sales Experience/Proven Track Record

Visit Appropriate Websites?

Currently Interviewing Elsewhere?

Are there any other offers on the table?

Timeframe for Availability to Start: ☐☐☐☐☐

Candidates Interest Level (1-10): Select One

Non-compete agreement?

CI Interviewing Questions

How important is it to you to be rated the #1 performer versus your peers? Why?

*Add all the add'l follow up questions.........

Competitive Drive Rating

Many people believe that it is better to do their best rather than to win or lose. How do you feel about that? *Add add'l questions.....

Driving Results Rating

Describe the situation that you feel best exemplifies your ability to bring creative, value-added solutions to your accounts? *Add add'l questions

Consultative Partnering Rating

Qualifying Questions: Give time for candidate to ask any questions they may have.

Client Company Review: If going to move forward, leave time to review Client Company a bit more in depth - go more into "sell" mode.

Closing Skills:
How did they close the call?

Candidate Summary:
Strengths:

Weaknesses:

Overall Score:

Sourcer Recruiter Interview Example (2):

Applicant Name : _____

Company/Position: _____

Recruiter Interview

YES   Applicant meets all requirements as specified on Job Order.

NO   Applicant has not met all requirements, yet is qualified to move forward with the interview process for the following reasons:

_____
_____
_____

Income Background :

Past 3 years w-2's :   Ever worked on commission only ?

Income level desired :

Interview Rating:
5 = Excellent Match, 4 = Great Match,
3 = Good Match, 2 = Acceptable, 1 = Unacceptable

____ Energy level / Enthusiasm   ____ Logical career progression

____ Well- Spoken   ____ Answers questions directly

____ Confidence Level   ____ Asks strong qualifying questions

____ Culture Match (independent/ entrepreneurial)
____ Overall phone presence
____ Integrity/honesty   ____ Other:

Comments :

_____
_____
_____
_____
_____
_____
_____
_____
_____
_____
_____
_____

Recruiter

Signature_____**Date**___

_____

__Forward   to   Recruiting   Manager   at **dobrien@salessourceinc.com** Please be sure to reference the company/position in Subject.

Face to Face Interview Example

Candidate:	Modality:	Territory:	Date:
(In walking thru resume-focus on candidate's experience in capital budgeting; hospital committee selling; sales cycles; #of accts they typically cover; prospecting methods; time management; databases they currently use; competitive knowledge in current industry; reasons for moves between jobs...	Score / Weight		Total
	Comments		
What has attracted you to this opportunity?			
Tell me about your dream job?			
College Background	Score / Weight		Total
	Comments		
What was your major? (change majors?)			
What school activities did you take part in? (Note activities listed on Career History Form and get elaboration,			
What was your GPA?			
What were high points during your college years? (Look for leadership, initiative, and			

particularly what competencies the interviewee exhibits now while discussing those years.)

Give me a feel for any jobs you held during college - the types of jobs, whether they were during the school year or summer, hours worked and any high or low points associated with them. (Don't spend too much time on these jobs, but look for indications of extraordinary initiative, motivation, etc.; if the person did not work during the summer, ask how summer months were spent.)

(TRANSITION QUESTION) What were your career thoughts toward the end of college?

Work History	Score	Weight	Total
	Comments		

What were your expectations for the job?

What results were achieved in terms of successes and accomplishments? (As time permits, get specifics, such as individual versus shared accomplishments, barriers overcome, "bottom-line" results, and impact on career - bonus, promotability, performance review.)

We all make mistakes - what would you say were mistakes or failures experience in this job? If

you could wind the clock back, what would you do differently? (as time permits, get specifics.)			
What circumstances contributed to your leaving? (Always probe for other reasons.)			
What was your supervisor's name and title? Where is that person now? May I contact him/her? (Ask permission to contact supervisors in the past ten years, in order to understand the candidate's developmental patterns.)			
What is your best guess as to what (supervisor's name) honestly felt were/are your strengths. Weaker points, and overall performance?			
Prospecting	Score	Weight	Total
	Comments		
Describe your system for prospecting			
How do you schedule appointments? How many a day/week?			
Is most of your prospecting by phone or in person?			
How much time and at what intervals do you set aside for prospecting?			
Qualifying	Score	Weight	Total

	Score	Weight	Total
	Comments		
In your current position, what are the 3 most important qualifying questions you ask before going for a demo?			
What would you foresee as some important qualifying questions to be for this particular position?			
Presenting	Score	Weight	Total
	Comments		
Using your current product as an example, give me your best presentation assuming that "I'm a busy doctor (decision maker) so you've got 2 minutes to tell me why you're better than the others.			
How do you overcome "your price is too high" objective?			
Tell me about the last customer you encountered that had a viable objection, and how you handled it.			
Closing	Score	Weight	Total
	Comments		
What is your most successful closing question?			
When was the last sale			

Question	Score	Weight	Total
you closed, and tell me how you closed it?			
Tell me of an example recently where you lost a sale.			
How do you go about following-up with most accounts?			
Personality	Score	Weight	Total
	Comments		
On a scale of 1-10, 1 being conservative and 10 being a risk-taker, where do you rate yourself? Why?			
If you were going to buy a stock today, would it be a GE or IBM type company, or some hot little Internet stock?			
What's the biggest risk you have ever taken professionally?			
If you were offered a job by GE Medical today, would you prefer to work for them directly?			
Tell me a few weaknesses that you have that you are trying to improve.			
On reviews with past managers of your sales performance, which things were brought up for you to work on, or to improve?			
Why are you in sales? Tell me about your first experience as a sales person.			
Empathy	Score	Weight	Total

	Comments		
You're on a blazing hot sale streak - everything you touch turns into a win. A conflict surfaces between a commitments you made weeks ago to attend an Opening Ceremony for a new Health Care Center featuring your new system and a last minute opportunity to crack that competitive account for a large order. Both are the same day, same time - neither can be rescheduled. What will you do?			
You have a good customer with a unique situation, and you honestly feel that for this particular need the competition has the better product for him and even at a better price. What would you do?			
Integrity	Score	Weight	Total
	Comments		
How would you define integrity?			
Explain the story of Pres. Club situation - changing PO - ask what they would do?			
Sales Scenarios	Score	Weight	Total
	Comments		

Use Visa/MC/AMEX scenario to test sales skills - look for how quick they assess the situation, how smart their 2 profiling questions are, how they sell and close.
Give telemarketing sales scenario - see how good they are when put on the spot. Look at their comfort level, confidence level, and overall presentation skills when they have to "wing it."
You walk into an account where they have been told by the tech that they have not seen a GE rep in years, and are strictly Siemens. What do you do?
Have you ever had an account that your predecessors told you were not worth your time, or this customer would not buy from your company - but that you did pursue and turned them around anyway? Or maybe some similar situation with incredible odds of landing a sale?
Let's assume that you are my last interview today, and I'm telling you that I'm going to hire another candidate because they have more experience, and I'm feeling stronger about them as a Fusion fit - how would you respond?
Describe a time that your company did not deliver and how you responded.

Follow-Up Questions	Score	Weight	Total

	Comments		
What drives you?			
What differentiates you from other people?			
If I had a management position I was hiring for as well, would you be more interested in that?			
How have you or would you manage a team of sales reps?			
What would you list as the most significant achievements in your life (Need not limit to professional life). What about professionally?			
If you could go back in time and do your career all over again, what would you do differently?			
Why did you choose that college/major? What was your GPA?			
How do you go about planning your days, weeks, and months? What kind of database do you use? (Try to see Daytimer - how they organize.)			
What are your short-term goals - personal & professional?			
What are your long-term goals - personal & professional?			
Why should I hire you?			
There are 10 people we are hiring for this sales team, if we hire you, where are you going to rank among the team in 6 months?			
	Score	Weight	Total

	Comments			
First Impression				
Energy Level				
Articulate				
Charisma				
Professional Appearance				
Confidence Level				
Friendliness				
Intelligence				
Entrepreneurial Spirit				
Positive Attitude				
Integrity/Honesty				
Tenacity				
Total	0	0	0	
Avg. Score	#DIV/o!	#DIV/o!	#DIV/o!	
A Player?				

Scoring Legend

5 = Excellent Match
4 = Great Match
3 = Good Match
2 = Acceptable
1 = Unacceptable

Questions from above:

Candidate: Modality:

To start, ask the candidate to give you a feel for any jobs they held in college- if they paid for college. What types of jobs did they doing during the school year or summer. Ask about hours worked, any high or low points associated with the various jobs. Don't spend too much time on these early jobs, but do look for indications of extraordinary initiative, motivation, entrepreneurialism, etc. If they did not work, as how they spent free time, or summers...ask about charitable endeavors, etc.

In walking thru resume- focus on candidate's experience in capital budgeting; hospital committee selling; sales cycles; #of accts they typically cover; prospecting methods; time management; databases they currently use; competitive knowledge in current industry; reasons for moves between jobs...

What has attracted you to this opportunity?
Tell me about your dream job?
College Background

What was your major? (change majors?)
What school activities did you take part in? (Note activities listed on Career History Form and get elaboration,
What was your GPA?

What were high points during your college years? (Look for leadership, initiative, and particularly what competencies the interviewee exhibits now while discussing those years.)

Give me a feel for any jobs you held during college - the types of jobs, whether they were during the school year or summer, hours worked and any high or low points associated with them. (Don't spend too much time on these jobs, but look for indications of extraordinary initiative, motivation, etc.; if the person did not work during the summer, ask how summer months were spent.)

(TRANSITION QUESTION) What were your career thoughts toward the end of college?

Work History

What were your expectations for the job?

What results were achieved in terms of successes and accomplishments? (As time permits, get specifics, such as individual versus shared accomplishments, barriers overcome, "bottom-line" results, and impact on career - bonus, promotions, performance review.)

We all make mistakes - what would you say were mistakes or failures experience in this job? If you could wind the clock back, what would you do differently? (as time permits, get specifics.)

What circumstances contributed to your leaving? (Always probe for other reasons.)

What was your supervisor's name and title? Where is that person now? May I contact him/her? (Ask permission to contact supervisors in the past ten years, in order to understand the candidate's developmental patterns.)

What is your best guess as to what (supervisor's name) honestly felt were/are your strengths. Weaker points, and overall performance?

Prospecting

Describe your system for Prospecting.

How do you schedule appointments? How many a day/week?
Is most of your prospecting by phone or in person?
How much time and at what intervals do you set aside for prospecting?

Qualifying

In your current position, what are the 3 most important qualifying questions you ask before going for a demo?
What would you foresee as some important qualifying questions to be for this particular position?

Presenting

Using your current product as an example, give me your best presentation assuming that "I'm a busy doctor (decision maker) so you've got 2 minutes to tell me why you're better than the others.

How do you overcome "your price is too high" objection?

Tell me about the last customer you encountered that had a viable objection, and how you handled it.

Closing

What is your most successful closing question?

When was the last sale you closed, and tell me how you closed it.

Tell me of an example recently where you lost a sale.

How do you go about following-up with most accounts?

Personality

On a scale of 1-10, 1 being conservative and 10 being a risk-taker, where do you rate yourself? Why?

If you were going to buy a stock today, would it be a GE or IBM type company, or some hot little Internet stock?

What's the biggest risk you have ever taken professionally?

If you were offered a job by GE Medical today, would you prefer to work for them directly?

Tell me a few weaknesses that you have that you are trying to improve.

On reviews with past managers of your sales performance, which things were brought up for you to work on, or to improve?

Why are you in sales? Tell me about your first experience as a sales person.

Empathy

"You're on a blazing hot sale streak - everything you touch turns into a win. A conflict surfaces between a commitment you made weeks ago to attend an Opening Ceremony for a new Health Care Center featuring your new system and a last minute opportunity to crack that competitive account for a large order. Both are the same day, same time - neither can be rescheduled. What will you do?"

You have a good customer with a unique situation, and you honestly feel that for this particular need the competition has the better product for him and even at a better price. What would you do?

Integrity

How would you define integrity?
Explain the story of Pres. Club situation - changing PO - ask what they would do?

Sales Scenarios

Use Visa/MC/AMEX scenario to test sales skills - look for how quick they assess the situation, how smart their 2 profiling questions are, how they sell and close.

Give telemarketing sales scenario - see how good they are when put on the spot. Look at their comfort level, confidence level, and overall presentation skills when they have to "wing it."

You walk into an account where they have been told by the tech that they have not seen a GE rep in years, and are strictly Siemens. What do you do?

Have you ever had an account that your predecessors told you were not worth your time, or this customer would not buy from your company - but that you did pursue and turned them around anyway? Or maybe some similar situation with incredible odds of landing a sale?

Let's assume that you are my last interview today, and I'm telling you that I'm going to hire another candidate because they have more experience, and I'm feeling stronger about them as a Fusion fit - how would you respond?

Describe a time that your company did not deliver and how you responded.

Follow-Up Questions

What drives you?

What differentiates you from other people?

If I had a management position I was hiring for as well, would you be more interested in that?

How have you or would you manage a team of sales reps?

What would you list as the most significant achievements in your life (Need not limit to professional life). What about professionally?

If you could go back in time and do your career all over again, what would you do differently?

Why did you choose that college/major? What was your GPA?

How do you go about planning your days, weeks, and months? What kind of database do you use? (Try to see Day-Timer - how they organize.)

What are your short-term goals - personal & professional?

What are your long-term goals - personal & professional?

Why should I hire you?

There are 10 people we are hiring for this sales team, if we hire you, where are you going to rank among the team in 6 months?

Characteristics to Score:

First Impression

Energy Level

Articulate

Charisma

Professional Appearance

Confidence Level

Friendliness

Intelligence

Entrepreneurial Spirit

Positive Attitude

Integrity/Honesty

Tenacity

Total

Avg. Score

A Player?

Scoring Legend

5 = Excellent Match

4 = Great Match

3 = Good Match

2 = Acceptable

1 = Unacceptable

Final Disclosure Interview

Final Disclosure interview to be provided by client. This covers review of compensation, start dates, benefits, etc. Everything should be reviewed and make sure nothing is left uncertain regarding the new position.

CHAPTER 4

WEEK 4: MARKETING

Marketing has been a theme in the past couple chapters, although it does deserve its own chapter dedicated to really breaking down the different areas you'll be marketing thru your day as a recruiter. From the first chapter discussing "You, the Recruiter," we started getting an understanding of how you have to start living like a recruiter, and then how to project that new image to the world, to make it real. This is marketing, and this will include tangible things like your business cards or website, to the more passive marketing that will take place on your phone calls in how you learn to market yourself or others. Remember the elevator speech we just worked on. The purpose of having a set paragraph to remember is to make sure you are hitting the most important points in best marketing yourself in the shortest time.

Elevator Speeches

The Elevator Speeches become go-to marketing sound bites for you when selling yourself to a new client, selling a client to a potential candidate, or when selling and marketing the candidate to your client. If you don't have a sales or marketing background, you may not even be aware that this was all marketing, however it's good to call a spade a spade. Even for those of you that don't like the idea of selling yourself, or marketing you and others. You have to understand that Marketing should be on your mind thru out the day, because this is now one of your biggest roles. Below I'll speak more to how you should best market yourself at these different levels, and hopefully, you'll start to incorporate a little marketing and a little selling thru out your day to help your business grow!

Marketing Yourself:

I'm lucky that I minored in Marketing at College, because it seems that a large part of the business world I have been involved in has been all about marketing. You start this journey needing to learn how to best market yourself. Whether that's thru your website, or thru the emails you send to clients or candidates, or straight thru to you marketing the candidate to the client. It's a sales game, and one that you need to understand. Marketing does matter. And although many people have very negative perceptions of sales and marketing, there is an art to it, and there are hard numbers and results that you will achieve by doing it properly.

So, what are some of the basics? First, and obvious, whether you've been a recruiter for years or just coming into this world after raising children for a decade or two, is that you have to remember to be professional. Look professional, speak professionally, and dress professional. Don't chat to your clients or candidates like friends. Yes, that comes later, but early on in the business relationship they are getting to know you, and they will need to trust and respect you to want to do business with you. This will be true for the candidate and client.

There could be an entire chapter on professional etiquette but for now, we'll stick to the marketing side of things. As a home based recruiter, you don't have to go too deep on the marketing side, unless you want to move onto larger accounts where you are wining and dining companies. I never really beefed up my SalesSource website until I needed something to prove to larger companies that I was a reputable business. Early on, I was just selling me, which is what you are kind of doing. Marketing is sales, and you will be marketing yourself and your recruiting skills. This will come thru in your phone conversations and emails, for the most part. Have a nice professional signature, and logo. This is easier than ever to create. Back in the day, it took lots of meetings, but so many things can be outsourced thru the internet now, that you can find people to help you online.

Often, a marketing plan or website, is as much about helping you define yourself, as it is about your client. Choosing your market place and thinking of who the audience is that you are marketing too are all things that will help you define what your business is going to look like.

Other than a business card, and a professional signature on emails, it's really about your personality coming thru the phone. I feel like I'm not giving too much credit to marketing here, but when you are starting up a small business like this, I think you could get too lost in the details of business plans and marketing proposals before you jump in. Obviously, a one pager is helpful to make sure you are focusing in the right direction, but after that, I recommend jumping in and getting your feet wet. You can figure a lot of the marketing out as you go, and as you discover ways of finding new clients.

Usually, the best marketing is done when you are calling or emailing searching for a candidate. When you are hiring managers and executive level people, you may often find that they are not interested in the job, but have hiring needs of their own. I found this out by accident early on, and used it to my advantage for years, uncovering new clients, while calling 'in search of candidates.' These were all legitimate job openings that I had, but I'll be the first to admit I would call certain manager for those jobs that I knew would not be interested, but were currently looking for people. Now a days, more than ever, you can find companies posting not only on their websites, but also on the job boards, as well as LinkedIn, and even Facebook today.

Although, most the marketing you'll do in the beginning is thru the phone or web, there may come a time where you must market yourself in person. For those of you just starting out, you may choose to skip this section, and just go onto the next topic of Marketing your Candidate. However, for those of you who can foresee themselves wanting to grow a client list thru live meetings of clients, or just to understand that world a little better, I'll expand here.

Conferences and Trade shows are a big part of marketing yourself and your business when wanting to grow. I use to attend these events back in my healthcare and medical days mainly to find candidates, as you can always find great candidates at the large shows. Especially in the sales market because the companies usually man their booths with their best sales people. The people that like to engage and speak to the people walking by.

The first few conferences I went to in my career were even before I had my own business. I think my first one was right out of college when I was looking for a new job, so in that instance I was the person I later sought out. Years later, when hiring for GE Medical, I would go to conferences to find the sales reps, as mentioned. Years after that, I went to find new clients for my business. I would also use the conference as a great time to catch up with current clients from across the country all in one place. I was hiring for a company called Hologic at the time out of Boston, SonoSite, a company based in Washington DC, Merge Medical, somewhere from the Midwest, along with several others spread thru out the country. I was able to go to one large show a year back then...the large RSNA held in Chicago at the McCormick center every year around Thanksgiving, and catch up with old colleagues, friends, clients, and make new ones, all over the course of a few days in Chicago. It became even more fun with a business partner, so we could tag team clients, and wine and dine new ones. I've been all over the country to conferences like this, and a couple out of the country. And most of them prove very beneficial.

In recent years, I've held an annual calendar of hitting the same Clean Technology conferences every year to bring in new business for the recruiting companies I consult for. Unlike, my healthcare days when I was only working clients for myself, one conference a year was enough to keep me busy at my desk all year. Not to mention, many of your clients come from contacts over the phone, even before meeting them in person.

With CleanTech, since I was drumming up new business for a new industry where I knew no one, I started going to a lot of conferences. I should again, give thanks to one of my mentors and CEO whom I worked with in Clean Tech- Andy Towne. I knew no one in the industry, nor did I know much about the market we were targeting- mostly all solar, wind, biofuel start-ups and the Venture Capitalists that could introduce us to more of those emerging companies. I remember my first cocktail party, trying to figure out among the sea of people, who to try and even talk to. Andy said, if you see the word, "Capital", on their name tag, it's usually a good contact. He was joking around, but also knew what he was talking about. He later taught me much of what I needed to know to understand the industry. I wasn't as productive as I thought I would have been that first year. I guess I had no idea how difficult it would be to jump into a new industry, especially in the 4th Quarter of 2008. But luckily, all those contacts I made later proved to be very worthwhile in my future, and I was able to bring some big wig clients to the table for the Partners to grow their business. One year later, at that same event, it was nice to hear my CEO tell someone 'new to the party' who asked a similar question of how to best network with the right people. He told that person to stick next to me for the event, as those were all the same people that I seemed to have luck in attracting and building fast relationships with. This person now runs his own VC firm in Canada, which I was happy to discover recently!

So, after figuring out the best conferences worth your time, you should simply make them an annual event. This way, you build your business around the events. It forces you to put out the marketing materials to potential clients before you go. You meet them while you're there, and the most important marketing is the follow ups you do within two weeks of getting back from the conference. I think I wasn't so successful my first year, because I had not learned that game yet. I didn't understand who was even sponsoring the events, which ones were good contacts, and how to best follow up. I learned, thru mentors, and thru trial and error, what seemed to work best, and then to simply cookie cut it.

To give you a basic idea, you'll look to go to the conference, and speak to as many people in your market at you possibly can. You want to collect their business cards, and follow up with all of them. Again, and I can't be more grateful to LinkedIn because they make this easier than ever. A quick LinkedIn invite is an easy way to follow up before you get a more detailed email out discussing your company, and how you would like to help them with recruiting needs. Out of 100 business cards you bring back, you'll probably have 10 strong leads, of which a couple should pan out in the short term. Others will play out more later. That's an overview of marketing yourself at the conferences.

I'll speak to more of this later, probably in an article geared to business development, more than headhunting. For purposes of this chapter, we'll focus more on you as a headhunter, which means you'll only need a couple clients to keep you busy behind your desk for the next year or more.

Marketing the Candidate

So enough on marketing yourself, let's turn to Marketing the Candidate.

Marketing the candidate will become a full time job from the moment you have a good one on the line. It starts when you send the resume, so be sure to spell check the resume for your candidate, or get rid of any issues before you forward their info to the hiring manager or Human Resources.

In the email that you send over to your client, you will want to be simple, concise, and to the point. Again, this will vary according to what your client may be asking you for, but generally speaking, thru the clients I've had over the years.. I should make a list one day, as I've probably forgotten half of them, but at least 30 clients or so in general, I can say the same thing.

Even if HR had certain processes that it wanted me or my recruiters to follow, typically my basic email forwarding over the resume was kept the same. It would have the resume attached, and a few simple bullets that matched the 'hot buttons' of my clients. For sales people, that may often be showing they were "President's Club Award Winners" for exceeding quotas, or Rookie of the Year, or any other proof of how good they were that I could get the manager excited about.

And that's the key- to get them excited about that person before their first conversation. And then to keep that momentum thru each phone call, meeting, and interview, until the offer is made. I should mention here too, that you are not only marketing the candidate, but you have to do your fair share of marketing the company also. So, although we've split these marketing topics into three different sections, you'll be doing these often all at once on your phone calls and emails.

Regarding the resume, not only do you want to spell check it to clean it up, but also add your company information to the header and footer. This speaks to always finding opportunities to market yourself, and also reminds whoever sees that resume, where they came from. If you don't have a company name yet, just put your name and number at the top and bottom.

Now, depending on the type of relationship with your client, you may sometimes remove the candidate's personal information. Especially if you are using a certain candidate to try and fish for new business. If you are sending a resume over before a contract is in place you should only have the person's first name and Last name's initial on the resume. Remove all personal contact info, and have your contact info clearly marked instead.

Obviously with the person's background on display, they could probably figure out who this person is, but hopefully they have higher values than that. At the same time, by taking the information off the resume, it will hopefully incent them to call you they like the background. Now, having said this, I personally have only done this a handful of times. Usually, I'm working with people I know and trust, and are almost always under contract before I send anyone there way. So, it hasn't been an issue for me as much. However, I have friend recruiters that use this method often, and since I've been known to do it a few times over the years, it's worth mentioning, so you are aware.

The email that you send is important, as I touched upon earlier. But so is the simple things like what you write in the subject line. Remember, this email could be going to an HR manager that receives 100 emails a day. Yours could easily get lost in the shuffle.

Although I respect your possible idea of getting creative in the Subject line, speaking from the position of an ex- HR Manager, I can tell you I appreciated the recruiters that helped keep me organized the best. I liked the candidate's name- the position- and location in the subject line. If I liked a job order referenced, I would tell them, and the recruiters that followed my instructions on this did not go unnoticed. Especially the ones that were consistent, and didn't get sloppy thru the months forgetting to put in simple things I asked for. So, knowing your audience, the first rule of marketing- make sure you are doing what your client wants.

Now, if you're sending this direct to the Sales Manager hiring the Sales rep, you may have more flexibility. I've been known to write, "Your next NYC rep- John Doe- resume attached!" to get his attention, although the HR Manager's email would be more by the book. And depending upon what I knew about the manager, I would customize my email message to incorporate the things I learned were most important to him when looking for a new rep on his team. This is where you want to keep just as good notes on your clients in your database, as you do on your candidates.

Marketing your Client

Although, the client has paid you, and you think of having to sell the candidate to them. If you are going to close the deal, you are going to have to sell the benefits of working for that particular company to your candidate from that very first phone call as well. Typically, your first phone call to the candidate, as we touched upon earlier, was not to interview them, but to get them on the hook. In the first few seconds of saying Hello, you have to quickly develop a report and say enough interesting things about this new opportunity to make them interested in hearing more. And just like doing this on the candidate side, you are continually playing matchmaker thru all steps until the deal is done. And if you're really good, you'll play a bit of a mother hen role during that first year to make sure they stick around at least one year, or else you could jeopardize your commission. A one year commitment should not be too much to ask, unless other circumstances come into play.

Keep in mind that although each client and company will have their own unique selling points, there are some basic things you'll need to make evident in that first call to a candidate to really get them interested.

Typically, the first thing you'll want to disclose is that the opportunity you are calling about is a step up in money from what they are currently earning. How do you know what they are currently making? You can often figure this out from learning your market and asking the right questions when interviewing other people at the same company. But also, you can often see their range of income on some of the job boards. It's always a good idea when hiring for a certain position that you call people that are maybe one position below in title. You want the job to be a step up in pay and title when possible. Title is not as important since titles can be thrown around, but they can sometimes serve as a good benchmark.

So, more money, better title, what else? Big company versus small company is important too. You should know that if you are hiring for a small, entrepreneurial company, it may be hard to attract someone with a track record of Fortune 100 companies. Now, having said that, the small company I hired for use to profile specifically for big company experience. Typically, in that situation we looked for someone with large company experience out of college, but no more than 5 years, and if they already chose to go to a smaller company after the large company experience, even better. So, I just mention this, so you learn to become very aware of who you are speaking to when calling some stranger to review a job. After money, job, company info, what else would be important in the first phone call hook. This should be somewhat a review from the 'Candidate Elevator Speech' chapter, but it's always good to review. So, otherwise, it's just about your energy and listening. You'll review some big points, and see if they'd like to hear more. You don't want to spend too much time marketing at this point, as you can let the company website and job description info you will email them after your call do more of the work for you. Yet, it's important to know these are some of the topics are when marketing the company, any company.

Week 4 Goal Checklist:

- ✓ Chapter 4: Week 4- Marketing Clients & Candidates
- ✓ This is a Numbers Game, Learn how to work the System
- ✓ Develop stronger system to where you see how the numbers work
- ✓ How many calls does it take to get a job order?
- ✓ How many calls does it take before finding a strong candidate?
- ✓ Are you controlling your day, or is your day controlling you? Review with mentor.

Diane O'Brien

Chapter 5

Week 5: Matchmaking & Send-Outs

Making the Match!

Week 5! Half way thru all this stuff you need to know about recruiting. I hope you're enjoying your days and weeks and although, it seems like a lot to learn, you'll be amazed how fast this stuff comes so easily in the months ahead. Now, we've covered all the Recruiting 101 details, the Clients, the Candidates, the Marketing, and now we're going to learn about Matchmaking between the different elements. This is where it gets fun. This is where you'll continue to use the marketing skills we discussed, and put your best foot forward.

I should also note that although, we've discussed Recruiting as an Art and a Science, there is a big X factor at play in this industry as well. No matter how well you've done your job, marketed, and interviewed, this job comes down to people's emotions, chemistry, and culture fits.

It's something you'll also get better with at time, but recruiting is so subjective, you cannot take it personal when the candidate you loved did not impress the CEO. Or when the candidate you thought was your backup person, or your "plan B" receives the offer instead. This will happen, especially in the beginning, when you don't know your clients that well, and are still learning how to read people better.

This is where trusting your gut instinct, and realize that you're a puzzle piece in a larger game. Do your job well, and you connect the right pieces of the puzzle. I often think when I'm searching for that "right candidate," or "the one," that there is one person that's meant for the job, and to try to research and investigate, and follow a referral path to find that person is the hunt. We are headhunters after all, and you're not just hunting any person, but the right one. All the marketing in the world doesn't make the match, it's finding the right match and them marketing them well, so they land the job.

So, just remember there's always a little mystery involved in this field, which in fact, has always kept it interesting to me. I never felt like I completely mastered this gig. I could successfully hire teams of great people, and feel very proud, but at the end of the year, find out that the one I thought would thrive quit, and the one that was a risk, ended as rookie of the year. So many circumstances affect this, so do your best, and let the cards fall where they are meant to be. Onto making that match and setting up the first face to face meeting between your candidate and client!

Send- Outs

After all the marketing on both sides, and figuring out if there may be a match, you'll be hopefully scheduling and setting up a lot of interviews face to face. We call this "send-outs" in the industry, and it's basically when you are sending out your candidate to go and meet the client. You want to get as many of your candidates thru the process and pipeline to get to this stage. The more qualified candidates you can send out, the more you increase your odds of making a match.

You want qualified candidates, but also want to be strategic in how you forward them onto the Hiring Manager. And although having 3 top choices would be ideal, you only need one to get the job done. So, it's always good to have a back-up, and if a third is in your pipeline, that's great. However, I typically found that whether I was hunting for a sales rep or VP, it usually came down to two good candidates when all was done. You send the best two forward, and hope you have a match. Usually, it worked out. Sometimes you have to go back to the drawing board which is a tough pill to swallow. But as you gain experience, your odds will increase, and more of your send-outs will match.

Be careful not to be like so many new contingent recruiters out there that just throw as many resumes and candidates at a company hoping that one sticks. You want to only send quality candidates. Its quality and not quantity in this game. There's tons of candidates that will want your job, especially in tough economic markets. However, your job as a good recruiter is to weed thru the junk for your clients, so you're only showing him your top guys and girls.

This is later what will truly differentiate you from other contingent recruiters, as well as retained ones.

In the future when you have multiple jobs that you are working at once, you should have a rough idea of how many send outs a week you would like to have to hit your goals. One a week was always a nice number for me, knowing that while you may be "in process" with other jobs, you would have face to face meetings happening as often as possible to close some deals.

Again, you'll find your own flow that can work consistently. Just remember to always watch the numbers. It is a numbers game, so you want to put the odds in your favor, especially since recruiting is so subjective. And if you are sending a manager to a certain city for a day of interviews, you would want to have a full day lined up, maybe as many as five. Usually after five live interviews, I start to burn out, and they all start running together. But if that's your one day to make a placement, stack up good, qualified people, to make sure they leave the day liking at least one, if not a couple.

Especially if this is a date close to some hiring deadline you may have to meet. Often, larger companies will have big training classes, and you need to get your candidates hired before that date, not forgetting to build in the two week notice time. So, when it comes to send outs, you don't always get a second chance. Depending upon the dates of when a manager is available to interview will help you determine the priority of what opening you are searching first.

Like much of what I discuss about working the plan backwards from the end goal, this is yet another piece where you do this. If you hiring for an opening in LA, and the manager will be there in two weeks, versus a newer opening in NYC, but the manager will be there next week- you learn where to shift priorities and manage your time to increase your odds of making the placement. I'll speak more to this later, especially when you get to the point of having multiple jobs and juggling multiple clients...that's where it get crazy, but fun!

Effective Conversations

If you're good at talking to people and having them open up to you quickly- you'll be in the right profession. You will also have to develop the other more detailed skills, but not get lost on the ones that won't matter at the end of the day. Knowing how to differentiate between the two is key. This is where another reading of Stephen Covey's "7 Habits of Highly Effective People" would be a good refresher. Separating the important tasks from the unimportant. Kind of getting back to you controlling your day in a very intentional way, and not letting the day control you.

When you have your phone interviews, the template will outline what you want to cover in a very concise, direct manner. I'm not saying that there's no room for casual chit chat. Especially, since that builds relationships, but be careful to keep it limited, and other than a couple casual remarks in the beginning, save that for the end, after you have someone on the line that you find out is someone you want to build a relationship with. There are people out there that when you catch them on their cell phone on a long drive, will keep on talking since they may not have anything else scheduled for that time. But you do. Whether you have another call coming in, or you have an interview coming up, so you need to cut the call short- don't be afraid, to give apologies, but express your need to have to run in a few minutes, so get right to the point.

Keep the conversations effective and focused. Get in to find out what you need to know, and offer them what you need to give, and then move onto the next. If you're not careful you can watch you day waste away in lots of interesting conversations, but you'll be no closer to filling your position. Take warning, and get good at staying on topic and on time.

God is in the Details & the Devil is in the Details

Have you ever noticed that some people say "God is in the Details," and other people say "the Devil is in the Details?" I fully understand how important the little details are in the recruiting process to make it go from a successful search to a failed one. And yes, it seems both God and the Devil are in different details. I suppose my interpretation of this, is that you do not want to get lost in the wrong details of the day, but you need to give special attention the important details of the day.

Overall, a good general rule that I have found is that when you are spending time with people, whether talking on the phone, or video conference, or a live, face to face meeting- these conversations and the little things said during those conversations, are the important details. Again, not spending too much time like we just discussed, but the time with people interacting is where you get a lot of the information needed to close a deal. Watching how a person's facial expression or certain pauses in a conversation seemed to always help me determine if they were the right fit, just as much as listening to their answers to my questions for over an hour.

Same with the resume, it wasn't really so much what was written on the resume, as much as all of the stuff that was "written between the lines". For example, when scanning a resume, I didn't get lost in reading every word, for that would be an example of the devil being in those details. However, I would look to see how long they have been at each job. I wouldn't focus on what they said they did, but look at the hard numbers of how they did. As a recruiter, you don't care so much that they worked 5 years for a great company with xx and yy responsibility. You will care about how much they increased quota, or improved company profits that year. Now, not everyone can write a great resume, so you will have to know the right questions to ask to get to the details that you want. Even though we're discussing details here, it's no secret by those who know me that I'm a very "broad-brush" kind of girl. Meaning I'm not the person that enjoys the small detailed paint by number. Give me large brushes, and I'd rather paint an entire picture, or get the general idea, instead of knowing all the details. I've always figured I'll figure out the details as they come.

This is both good and bad, but I think just part of how I'm wired, and has been useful as a recruiter since it could be so easy to get lost in the details, with mass resumes, and mass callbacks, and conversations to hit a deadline. Keeping your eye on the ball, and of the overall game and goal is key.

If you are similar, it's good in the area of moving your business forward, and doing the important tasks thru out the day. You hopefully wouldn't get lost in silly details that won't matter anyway.

Yet, you'll need to be sure to take your time in the other important areas. Luckily for me, although I don't like details, it's more the details on paper or following directions. I do like the details in getting to know people and seeing what makes them tick, and those kinds of things. I still enjoy finding those answers about myself as I grow older. And learning the details of someone you love can keep you interested for a lifetime. So, luckily the details in life that I deem important work well to the role of recruiter.

Utilize your Mentor- Don't reinvent the wheel!

Spending time with someone and asking the right questions to get to the right answers is fun for me. It should be fun for you too. Especially, if you are planning on being a recruiter. Now, details like accounting and bookkeeping, or paperwork- I'm really bad at. I've learned the hard way to leave that to professional accountants, or assistants, so I can focus on what I'm good at.

In bringing up assistants, I should mention to be careful when trying to get certain details off your desk that an assistant can handle, I made the mistake of having scheduling be one of those tasks. I later realized, that unless your assistant is well trained as a recruiter, you could lose a deal if you're not the one helping schedule calls.

When my sourcer/recruiter helped schedule- that would be fine, because she was also incented to close the deal, and was very good at reading cues when finding out if someone was running late, or plane delays happened, and then how to properly communicate that to the hiring manager. A general secretary however, or a shared assistant doing the scheduling will often miss important details during these important "touch-points," that could cost you a placement. It's happened to me, and I can give several examples on this to discuss to make sure you don't make those same mistakes. This, again, is where a good mentor can help guide you in your process, and what you should or should not be focusing on.

Scheduling

Since we just left off on this topic of scheduling, let's cover this detail a bit more. You will be scheduling conversations to take place thru your day. People's time is very valuable, and so is yours. And you'll find that the higher up the ladder you climb when interviewing candidates or clients, often the tougher it may be to get on their schedule, if you're not lucky enough to just happen to catch them on their cell phone. I love those lucky moments.

Good luck meets Opportunity while "Scheduling"

My favorite story here was for a CFO at Beth Israel Hospital and NYC when I was a sales girl. I was on the train from Philly to NY, and really needed the CFO's buy in on purchasing new software for their imaging department. I called his cell number, he actually answered, and when I mentioned I was on the train coming to his hospital (which wasn't the reason for my trip, as I had other accounts I was visiting), the phone started to break up, so he just gave me a time to meet him that afternoon. I was able to get in for the unexpected meeting that day, and walked out of the hospital with a purchase order. It ended up being one of the first purchase orders for my team, and brought me a lot of accolades. And proved to be a good lesson in getting someone live time on the phone.

If I would have left that call to an assistant, it never would have happened. This example was from my sales days however. Let me explain more on the recruiting side. When you have someone strong, and you are setting up the first phone call or meeting, you need to set up both parties of "what to expect" to make this a "warm meeting" and not a "cold meeting." Often, the more they already know about the other person from you helps them connect quickly, and get on to business, instead of going thru the first awkward formalities. This info can be communicated once again on your last phone conversation to each before the meeting. Whether it's the night before, or if you're speaking to them as they are coming off the plane. You are the quarterback of this game, and you have to help bring it home. You are connecting them, and want to make sure the connection goes smooth. Also, scheduling problems will come up. People are late, planes are late, traffic happens, etc. How you communicate this to the manager can impact his first impression. I once had a manager not even give a candidate a chance because she was 10 minutes late due to crazy weather.

He just thought that meant rain, which wasn't excusable, but there were overturned trees and down wires, with detours that made her late. Now, yes, we can all argue you should leave ample time for an interview, but life happens. Heck, when I was interviewing for a sales job at Pfizer, I went the wrong way on the Pennsylvania Turnpike and was hours late. I'm still amazed I got the offer, but they were impressed I didn't give up, and remained calm and collected thru my interview, after apologizing for my mistake.

If my recruiter never called them to explain why I was late, they may not have been open to seeing me. But as a recruiter, if you can help give the "back-story" on anything, it helps build the bridge you're trying to build between these two parties. This happens at each step, from the first phone call, to the first meeting, to the last meeting, to the offer letter. Keep the scheduling as one of your important tasks, and if you need to take on an assistant later, she'll have to be in sync with this and hopefully tied financially to the outcome.

Week 5- Goal Checklist:

Week 5- Matchmaking & Send-outs

✓ Review Chapter 5
✓ Draft sample email to client- forward to mentor
✓ Draft template email for 'Candidate Prep checklist'
✓ Have Scheduled times for candidate prep (20 minute call)
✓ Have Scheduled times for client confirmation (20 minute call)
✓ Draft template for scheduling confirmations
✓ Review process for send out- Phone, Face to Face, Final Interviews

Diane O'Brien

CHAPTER 6
WEEK 6: SIX SIGMA PROCESS

Week 6, and we're moving down the process. Having reviewed all of the steps in the process from getting the job order to now connecting the client and candidate together, we must look closer at this process. You cannot really get a good feel for how this all comes together until you do it yourself a couple times. But after a while, perhaps a few months, and a couple closed deals, you'll realize there's a system to this, just like anything. If you follow certain steps, you can break this mysterious world of recruiting into tasks and numbers. Take into account some room for error, but you'll have a system that you can cookie cut over and over.

An old manager use to explain it as "cracking the code." Every job can be broken down to process, and if you can manipulate that process in a way to achieve success most of the time by following certain patterns, your job as a recruiter will become easier, and you'll feel more in control. This is where we get to studying the Process of Recruiting, and constant process improvement to get you to the next level.

Six Sigma

I truly do give a lot of credit to big company training, because even though, at the time, I thought many of the training courses were a waste of my time, I really did learn a lot from them, and use many of those lessons today.

One of my favorite courses was GE's six sigma process training. I still have that training binder somewhere that first made me think about the "process improving" my job. I graduated as a green belt- probably meaning I passed, but was still pretty green! My husband did the full black belt training, and I think he would also say that it served him well.

So, basically it's all about process improvement. Everything we do can usually be broken into a process, and the better you get at the process, and the more you can find ways of improving that process, the better you will be. In business terms, this means you will make more money in less time, and in life terms, this means you can get more done faster, thus giving you the free time to do whatever the heck you wish to be doing.

Recruiting, although it is also very much an Art, and can be very subjective when it comes to picking the right people, it is still a process that can be broken down into set timelines. Now, different job orders can take a different amount of time, generally speaking. So this process may be cut to weeks if you're hiring a temporary person, to months if you're hiring a VP. I'll speak to my experience which was the six figure jobs in general, starting with high end sales professionals and going to Managers, VP's or CEO's.

The 8-12 week time frame always proved pretty sufficient. It took a couple weeks to find the right candidates, it took a couple weeks in the client's court to speak and meet with them. Add a couple weeks for another meeting and final interview. And add a couple more weeks for the 'two week notice' and add a couple weeks for error, such as rescheduling, or other delays. Scheduling really eats up the time, as you try to connect people. If everything was done immediately, you could place someone in a few weeks right after finding them. But even though, your job of hunting the right person may have been fulfilled in week one or two, the client takes longer than they think they will in meeting the candidate and scheduling the final interviews. Even when utilizing video conferencing to cut out travel time, we would still recommend a live meeting before an offer goes out, so all this takes time. Usually week by week. I'll add the process plan that I used at my company SalesSource to show you how it kind of looked.

Again, as technology changes, this may speed up, but people can only move so fast. You can figure out how you're process typically goes, and try to improve it as much as possible. It also seems that this time frame was also needed for a person to make a mental jump from one job to the next. From the first phone call where you call them, out of the blue, offering a potential position. Usually, these are happily employed people not looking to make a move. They want to research, meet the people at the new company, have several conversations with you and them, and sleep on it for many nights. Have the weekends to talk to their spouses about the potential move. I have found that this takes time, regardless of how fast technology can move us. And the bigger positions, with more money at stake, take more time to really investigate for the candidate. It's a big deal changing jobs, and all this take time. The better you understand the realistic timelines, the more control you'll feel over your days and weeks.

The Recruiting Process Review

I've taught this concept to many clients, as well as helping candidates in play understand what the road ahead would look like. I have yet to meet a Hiring Manager that doesn't think you can get a job order today, and have the candidate hired next week. Even the experienced Managers seem to forget the basics. I've recruited for many of the same Managers over time, and many of them would still ask for the same job description with the same timing, of needing someone asap, which could mean by training in 2 weeks.

I've tracked the process and maybe it was my 'greenbelt' process improvement training when I was at GE after college, but from my first day I would track the process, and the steps didn't change much whether they requested a hire tomorrow or in a month. The time it takes to find a person and get them hired is pretty set. Like anything, there are exceptions, but as a rule- this is the timing. And if you educate your clients on this (tread lightly in these areas not to come off like you know more than they do), but if you get them on the same page- they will match the time table you outline to make for the most successful hiring campaign. Especially if you're helping them hire an entire team at once, which had been my specialty for most of my years as a recruiter.

Recruiting Process & Timelines

We touched upon this earlier, but it's safe to generalize recruiting at this level, as an 8-12 week process. Be careful how you phrase this because you don't want to give the wrong impression that it will take you two months to find and help hire the person. The timing is split down the middle. From the day of job order- the ball is in your court for 1-3 weeks as you find, screen, and schedule the candidate with client.

Week 3-6 is in the client's court. I think you'll find scheduling is the biggest time taker, and obstacle in getting your person hired quick. Trying to get a phone interview time that matches your client and candidate schedule usually takes a week...that's was air travel. Since I recruited nationally, this was the case 90% of the time, and this would happen around week 5. Then, the final should occur by about week six. Two weeks for your typical 2-week notice takes you to a start date by week eight, if lucky.

See attachment (Typical Recruiting Process) of the typical outline to really make sure you understand the process. Also, remember that you don't get paid until 30 days after the start date. So although the actual process from start to finish is around 8 weeks- You really won't see that check until several months later. This is where it's important for you to have realistic expectations on how you grow your business. And make decisions on how many jobs you can do effectively at one time to create a funnel that will keep income coming in on a monthly basis, ideally.

Selling People, not Product

We're not just selling product here, we are moving people. Moving families sometimes across the country, for a new job that you have offered. At least a good month seems to be needed, 4 weeks of digesting the idea, before a candidate makes the move.

Think about your own life, when changing a job. How long did it take you from the first recruiter phone call to accept an offer? A couple weeks would be very fast, unless there were other circumstances at play. Three to four may be more average. Perhaps a couple more for higher positions. But remember you had the two weeks needed on the front end with all the hunting of the right person, as well as the two weeks on the back end to give proper notice. So, this will be your timeline in general. At least if you're hiring in a similar market to what I have done.

Pushing Job Order to Close

As we've discussed in previous chapters, pushing your job order thru is a bit of an art. You can't push too hard or you'll annoy the client, and you can't go too light or you could jeopardize the deal. You are definitely the quarterback of this process. This is the reason companies' need recruiters- not just to find the candidate, but to be the "mother goose" of the candidate until they sign the offer letter. And also to be the consultant to the client to help make sure their moving the process along. Strong candidates may have other job offers, and it's your job to make sure nothing pops up at the final stages that would have the closing fall thru.

It is crucial that you are very sensitive and insightful during each conversation that you have with the client and candidate at each step of the process until the deal is done. This makes and breaks many placements, and you'll need to finesse this skill as early as possible. Keep in mind, your approach will change depending on the client and the relationship that you develop with them. As you place more candidates at their company, their confidence will typically grow in your ability, and you'll be able to gain more trust, which allows you to be more direct.

Becoming a trusted "Recruiting Partner"

This is when you feel more like a true consultant and partner in helping them grown their business thru making the right hires. Your client will hopefully look to you, not as a typical recruiter, but a true partner that cares about them and their business, even more than just making a short term placement. The best salespeople and the best recruiters truly do care about the clients and their interests. I've known CEO's of recruiting firms that would take on business they knew they could not complete, whether due to lack of manpower or industry knowledge. This is not a sustainable plan, and the good ones learned fast that it's better to turn down a job than ruin your reputation trying to fill it.

Candidates Comes First

In the beginning, when you are very hungry for a placement and you may not know the customer very well yet- it can be tempting to try and simply close the deal. However, I believe it is the human element of thinking of your client first that will ultimately differentiate you from all the other wannabe recruiters out there. In fact, putting others needs before your own, will often differentiate you in a good way, in life in general, so it's a good rule to follow. I have personally lost deals by recommending my client "not" hire a person that I may have recommended earlier, but later gained more insight into that person's character. I may have lost that specific placement, but gained a long term client. Integrity in the deal should be a non-negotiable. In the same way you should always put people before money, you should also put your values and integrity before money as well.

This is the best way to ensure long lasting, sustainable success in your career. Remember, you can have 10 success stories with a client, but if there's one deal that goes bad, this is what they'll often remember, so be sure to keep the integrity of the search and relationship paramount.

Client Chemistry

Similar to pulling back the reins on a search due to the candidate not being right, I have also stopped working with well-paying clients, if I feel they are not up to par. You may have a great company for a client, but that doesn't mean all of the Hiring Managers you will hire for within that company are people you are going to like. I realize early on, you may have to suck it up, if this is simply a personality clash, but if it's something more regarding the Hiring Manager or the job itself, I feel it my duty to follow my gut. In the same way that you develop relationships with clients, you also develop strong relationships with candidates. Sometimes, you may even place the same candidate two or three times during their career. I found it very difficult if I had to replace a sales rep in a certain territory that I believed was a "bad" territory, versus a "bad" rep.

Companies may try to glide over the fact that the territory has issues, even after they replace multiple people in the job. It didn't take me long in certain situations to say no to certain job orders where I believed having a person move their family to another part of the country would not be a good move, in the long run. Back to the golden rule thing, I suppose. I wouldn't want someone ever selling me a bill of goods that wasn't accurate to simply turn a buck. If it doesn't feel right, the money is never worth it, and I have more than one story of proof within my recruiting business to prove that what goes around, does indeed come back around.

One of my favorite stories is with a good candidate that didn't get hired, and I stopped working the job because I knew she was the right one for the job. There were more than questionable reasons why she did not get hired. I had back up candidates that could have easily replaced her, and I could have made my $10k fee at the time, but I decided to walk away instead, leaving the territory open. The company spent months continuing a search, but eventually made changes to the territory, which was around LA. This made it more lucrative and travel friendly for the reps. Less than one year later, I was able to place that same girl in a now improved territory.

The best part, was that I re-negotiated my contract with my client during that time, and made $13,500 for that placement, $3500 more than my original contract the year earlier. It felt like an instant reward for doing the right thing. If I would have listened to my client, or the desire for money at that time, I would have probably spun my wheels for months, wasting time and money. Instead, by following my gut, and putting my attention elsewhere, it all came back around for the best. It always feels good to look back with 20/20 vision and know you made the right choice. Granted, there will be times, when you look back, and feel like you made the wrong choice. But most of those times simply serve as learning experiences anyway. We're all just a work in progress in this life, ever evolving, so don't beat yourself up if you learn some of these lessons the hard way.

In summary, closing the deal is not just about seeing the job thru to the end, but closing the deal in a manner you can be proud of. So, when the checks roll in the mail, and you want to celebrate, you're not only celebrating the money that may give you some of the material things you desire, or financial security you are trying to achieve, but also a celebration of you staying true to who you are. By making sure not to bend to the world's whims or what paying clients tell you, but by closing the deal in a way where you know everyone wins- this will sustain you, and move your career forward into new levels thru out your life.

More on the Process

You'll have two Processes going on that you will watch. First, you will have the general outline of the typical recruiting process, which may follow an 8-12 week process, as outlined. Like we discussed, this could be shortened to days for temporary positions that move fast, or stretched to months for C-Level positions, such as CEO's or VP or Director Positions. However although the time line may vary, the process will usually follow the same steps. Now, in my experience from selling sales reps to CEO's, this has held true. After consulting for different CEO's and companies that often hired outside my expertise, I know this may vary. The point will be to figure out whatever the typical process looks to be, write it down, and find ways to improve it.

Maintaining Balance

When I first started recruiting, I don't know if it was being young, or simply inexperienced in recruiting, but looking back, I'm amazed I filled as many jobs as I did. I was so crazy busy, it was like that fast moving bus example, where you don't have time to slow down to fix the tire, or fix something that urgently needs fixing. Like anything in life, when we're not proactive, or delay in something that's important, the small simple weed, could turn into a larger problem that won't take two minutes to pull from the ground. Instead, the small problem grows to where it will take days or weeks to fix. Funny...I don't know why I just gave a gardening example. It annoys me when men use sports analogies for everything- did I just use a gardening analogy? Well, hopefully you get the point.

Anyway- stop your busy day, to plan the right way to do things. When you first start putting calls out to candidates, you will feel like your spinning your wheels. Then, all of a sudden, hundreds of calls or emails are coming back to you. Emails with resumes attached and awaiting your response, or phone calls from people you forgot you reached out to, awaiting more information on the job that you've know raised their interest in. Just wait until you have 10 jobs, and between candidates calling you back, or old clients, vs. new clients, you're process can go crazy very quickly. So, if you start living your day, the way you would if you already had 10 clients and 100 candidates to shuffle, you'll make wiser decisions of where to spend your time and where not to spend it.

I think this is one of the most important decisions we make hundreds of times a day. Do I give this my time and energy? And if yes, when is the best time. Now, or later. Never losing sight of the big goal for the day. Otherwise, even without all the distractions of phone calls and emails from people wanting your time, the daily life stuff like the bills, or laundry, or a car repair, or calls from friends...will end up unwinding your day. Instead, plan time for all of these things, along with your work. When you get good at this, your work day runs smooth.

And I should point out there, that this is probably a never ending process, because just when I think I've mastered it, an entire new endeavor falls in my lap that may threaten to jeopardize it all. Just as I got my life organized around my recruiting business, SalesSource, I jumped into the world of Business Consulting in a new industry with lots of travel, and my old process had to crack a bit. And then from there to mentoring or adding charitable responsibilities- that put another kink in my schedule too. And rental properties with property managers, or pool service guys, contractors, kids schedules, doctors....just writing all this is probably raising my blood pressure.

I can tell you though, when I go into my office, and close those doors, my work does become my sanctuary. I do control my business, those hours, and the money I make. That world is often easier to keep straight, than my personal world at times with kids, husband, pets, homes, and stuff always going on. And I won't even bring up typical marriage issues. I only wish I could have a six sigma process map for making marriage go according to set goals. If I could write that book, that would be a true miracle. For now, teaching the basics of how to earn six figures recruiting from home, is good, since I've been there and done that, and have taught others how as well.

Sorry to get off subject, but considering many of you are similar to me, I think it's probably important for you to know that I have all the same "distractions" as any of you. If I have been able to do this, then so can you. If that's what you really, really, want. So, again, as you continue on this journey, make sure your walking the right path for you. I've said it before, and I'll say it again. If you're only reading this because it's a path to make lots of money...that's not a good enough reason. If this sounds fun, exciting, and something that you would love to do, regardless of the money...you're on the right track. The good news is that recruiting pay days are very nice, so for the right ladies- this job is perfect. It so exciting to open up this world to some of you who may have not known much on recruiting. There's a lot to it, and a lot of money to be made. And the best secret is there are so many of us doing it from home.

Week 6 Goal Checklist- Process & Pushing Job Order to Close

- ✓ Read Chapter 6
- ✓ Maintain Scheduled calls continuing to develop pipeline for future biz
- ✓ Review Touch points- follow up calls to client and candidate
- ✓ Preparing file for back up candidates

Week 6 Attachments:
Process Outline- 8-12 week outline.

Recruiting Process Example:

Recruiting Process- 8 week time line per opening:

First 3 weeks- Sourcing/Pre-Screening

1. Hiring Manager completes Job Order Form.
2. Submits Job Order to Recruiting Manager for approval.(phone conversation making sure it's a real order to hire, have appropriate attachments- territory info/acct. list)
3. Job Order is sent to 1- 2 Recruiters (depending on volume/territory).
4. Recruiter will call HM to review Job Order- get any questions answered.
5. Recruiter starts search, and preliminary screening process begins. (takes 1-2 weeks)
6. Recruiter presents 3-5 candidates by emailing resume and Recruiter Interview   Form to HM (weeks 2-3).
7. HM reviews candidates, and arranges with Recruiter to speak to the top 3 by phone (weeks 3-4)- 1hr phone screens.

----------Hand off from Recruiters to Managers------

Second 3 weeks- Interviewing/Hiring:

8. *HM conducts phone screens- narrows down to 1-2 to meet F2F. HM/Recruiter schedules date for F2F meeting (weeks 4-5).
9. **HM conducts f2f interview- narrows down to 1 candidate to make offer.
10. HM completes New Employee Request Form to generate offer letter- sends to ?ask CFO.
11. ***HM brings candidate in for Final Disclosure/Position Agreement, to meet with any other Parties (CEO, Hiring Managers)and to make job offer. (week 6)
12. Candidate accepts/signs offer letter, gives 2 weeks' notice- determine start date.

Last 2 weeks- Hiring/Retaining

13. Candidate start date- Manager should call (week 8)
14. 90 Day check –

*Touch points between you and candidate (currently 3 with Hiring Manager)
Who is calling to arrange travel, hotel, limo service- Admin? (Should only be one more)
Client contact at this point- the Hiring Manager and the travel coordinator.

Other Process Examples:
(This one for a new manager to follow Hiring Timelines)

Manager Interviewing PROCESS Checklist

- Submit Job Order with territory map and account list to Recruiting Manager

- Conduct 30 min-1hr phone interviews with candidates
  (See phone interview)

  - Follow-up with Recruiter/Candidate, arrange next step

  - Conduct 1-2 hour Personal Interview with select candidates (see Personal Interview)

  - Follow-up with Recruiter/Candidate, arrange next step

  - Conduct Final Interview at office, reviewing Final Disclosure and making offer.
    Have Divisional Manager included if wanted.

  - Make official offer, verbally and written.

  - Explain to candidate that the offer is contingent on the following next steps to be done over the 2-week notice before their start date:

  - Meet the Manager
  - Conduct CI Profile

- Background Checks; Additional Reference Checks

- Call the candidate during this 10-day lapse, and on their Official Start date.

Recruiting Process- Hiring Manager & Recruiter

Our Mission:
The goal of Fusion's Recruiting Department is to recruit at a world-class level.
To develop a recruiting model and process that would work successfully for 1 opening or 100 openings.
To work within the existing process to get the job done, while always keeping a key focus on process improvement.
To find, screen, hire and retain top-level sales people in a timely fashion at a good value.
To recruit with the highest level of integrity.
To promote a Recruiting culture within Fusion that will provide us with the highest caliber sales rep at the very best value.

How do we reach our goal? With a clearly defined plan (see new recruiting model and process), with awesome teamwork, and with measurements.

"United we stand, divided we fall"
Recruiting is a team effort between the Recruiter and the Hiring Manager.

To Find>>>Recruiter
To Screen>> Recruiter/Manager
To Hire>>>Manager/Recruiter
To Retain>> Manager

The Recruiting Manger's role will be to manage the entire 8 week process, making sure both parties are keeping the commitments necessary to make a quality placement on time.

Recruiter>>>>>>Recruiting Manager<<<<<<Hiring Manager

To present 3-5 quality candidates. To hire the best candidate within 3-4 weeks of the initial phone interview.

Recruiting Model Example-

The New Recruiting Model (Plan Example)

Recruiters - the do'ers- find A players within 3 wks
Need 2 Recruiters per business (GE, Agilent, IBM, Tyco,-9 currently)
     Output: 10-20 placements per year

Sr. Recruiter/Recruiter Liaison - high paid do'er-$80K little mgmt skills
     ----- **do** the process, and some level of management.
Would handle all internal referrals, call ins, web resumes, direct sourcing, scrubbing
Database, monster. Could manage one business with 2 recruiters- GE?
Output: 20-40 placements per year (what we've done previous 2 yrs)

*Recruiting Manager -More managing (thinking) skills-$120K
     -----**manage/improve the** process (can   manage   4-6 recruiters/sales mgrs successfully)
     Could manage the recruiting process for 2-3 Fusion business- Agilent/IBM
     And manage 1-2 Senior Recruiters
     Output: 40-60 placements per year *What I think we need now?

Human   Resources   VP/   HR   Director- highest   paid thinker/manager- $150K.
     -----Improve the process extremely well (can manage 1-2 Recruiting Managers)
     Output: 80-120 placements per year *What CEO says we'll need

Entrepreneur /Intra-entrepreneur ----creates the process; 'cracks the code'-$200K
Next level- do it over again$$ and start to inspire future entrepreneurs

     *Someone smart enough to pull herself out of the day to day details, to envision the ideal recruiting model that would work successfully for 1 opening or 100. To work within the existing process to get the job done, while always keeping a key focus on process improvement to do the task of Recruiting: To find, screen, hire, and retain top level sales people in a timely fashion at a good value.

Need to agree on what that means, something we can measure:
Top-level sales people- A Players- 2 measurements
    A. Deliver 1-2 A's w/in 3 weeks (recruiters control)
    B. Hire and Retain past 90days (managers control); need to train mgr on process first, interview skills later...
Timely fashion- 6-week hire from day of job order.
    A. 3 weeks to help recruiters deliver an A
    B. 3 weeks to help managers make the hire
Good Value- Mgrs (15-20%) flat rate $18-20K
        Sales reps (8-10%) flat rate $8-10K
        Rates subject to change depending on market place

The Unknown: We can be successful in this role handling up to ? placements per year?
What's the value in creating this new process?
Expectations?

Diane O'Brien

Chapter 7

Week 7: The Seven Week Itch

You've got a solid job in play, and after your hurry up and now wait on feedback from that job- you have time to focus on getting more jobs going. The more jobs you work, the more send outs you have, the more placements you will make. Again, this is a numbers game, so control what you're putting in to make sure you get what you want out. At this point, you're basically starting over the same old process. Everything you learned from week 1, Chapter 1, on how to get a job order and doing it all over again.

Sustainable Process

The great thing about this, like anything else, is that once you do it one time, you know you can do it again. It can seem like a mountain to climb, especially when you haven't even closed your first job yet. You've put in numerous hours, and here you go again without a penny to show. But this part of the game, the part that seems to separate those of great faith versus those of little faith, becomes the true proof of the pudding. Most people give up at this stage, because they listen to that small voice telling them that it's all a waste of time. You may hear that same voice telling you that this work won't amount to anything of real value, and if you let that voice keep going, it will steal your thunder, steal your energy, and steal all the good things that await you. This is the very reason that most people reading this book that try to become a successful recruiter, will not be able to. It most likely will not be that they don't have the skills or the time, it will typically be that they don't believe they can do it, so they don't. Or they are afraid to try and fail, so they think it better not to try at all. Please, don't be one of those people. I'm guessing the 80/20 rule applies here, and 80% will quit. You need to be the 20% that have faith and push thru.

So, no, you have not been validated yet by the outside world, in the form of a fat pay day. You're only validation is believing in yourself that you want to do this, and that you can do it. And you will continue to invest time to make your dreams come true. No one else is going to make them come true for you, right? Many of us ladies have banked on someone else making us happy, and how does that usually work out for us? It's great to have your loved ones, spouses, family, and friends add joy to our life, but by the end of the day, who makes you happy and fulfilled. I'm guessing that's more between you and your God, than anyone around you.

Anyway, I know I go off topic at times, but the message to get here on Week 7- let's call it the "7 Week Itch", is to not throw in the towel, and give up. Push thru. Start the process over, find another client. Get that job order. Start hunting for candidates to present. Work that plan, and the job.

Also, remind yourself that you signed up for a ten week plan, and we're only at week 7, so even if you want to give up- I hope you would honor your commitment, and then at week ten, if you think it was a mistake, you can at least hold your head high, knowing you gave it your all. If it becomes apparent that you would not enjoy the recruiters day to day, then okay, this book has helped you rule out another career. But, if this does sound like a good fit, and your talents seem in line with these qualifications, do not give up. See this thru for at least ten weeks. You can crash course this, and learn the info in ten days. You can even, not take any action, and just read this book in a couple hours, but to really implement this lifestyle, and to become a recruiter, you need the next ten weeks to make this real. Week seven will be tough because you've invested some time at this point, with nothing yet to show. Get to week ten, and run the process thru with a client or two, then decide. Perhaps you'll find your niche job within the different aspects of recruiting. I'm teaching a gig where you can do all facets from home, but maybe later you learn to like one part, and partner with an outside recruiting firm to help them from home. You could be the researcher, you could be their recruiting coordinator, or the interviewer, or maybe the business developer meeting the clients. You don't know until you try, so make sure not to throw out all of this work, until you know where it may play out for you in the long run.

The Seven Week Itch- Don't give up!

There's a reason you're reading these words today, so have faith and put it to use. Even if this takes on a path to be an entrepreneur in another field....sometimes you can get inspiration from places you wouldn't expect that trigger some long time desire. Nothing inspires me more than watching other people live out their own dreams. And it goes both ways. If I'm looking ahead to a mentor I respect, and would like to 'live a similar life' to the one I see them live- they inspire me, and I learn from them how to get there. Just like they were giving me a road map. Same is true when I mentor women coming up in the recruiting world behind me. If they can see what I've created, and I can give them a book on "how to" do this, it takes away much of the mystery of how to be successful in any given career. If you haven't already thru this journey, I encourage you this week, more than the others, to take a deep breath. Look at where you came from, look at where you want to go, and really sit in the moment of where you are. Let yourself feel any fears or any hope that resides in you. Listen to your voice deep in you telling you if this is the right path, or if this is a temporary path to get you on the right track. You may decide to stop here, and go where you need to go, or decide you cannot wait to make your first placement. Listen to your gut. Thru the first few months of my business, although I felt fear, my desire to get that first placement trumped the fear. If that's where you sit, keep going. If not, that's okay too...do some more soul searching.

So, how long before you can take that deep breath? I can tell you this- with all of the companies and clients that I've worked with over the years, one thing remains the same. The ramp up period to learn something new. Although we're discussing this as a ten week program, if you were to start any new job, three months, or twelve weeks, is usually the amount of time to get an idea of how you are doing. Six months becomes a very strong indicator of how well you are picking up new material and utilizing it all. For many of the training sessions I went thru as a sales girl at Fortune 100 companies like GE, or SmithKline, they would offer training at the start, and then often wait to train again 3 months in, and 6 months too.

This really helped make sure you were absorbing everything. And to be honest we really never knew who the superstars were really going to turn out to be until usually the one year mark. In fact, forget superstar, even to make sure the employee would stick around for a year. If they made it past the one year mark anniversary, chances are that they were a good fit. So, I say this for a couple reasons. First, be easy on yourself while learning all this new information, and realize that although you are pushing hard for the next 10 weeks, it's the next 10 months or so that will help you realize you made the right choice. I also mention this, because this is why most recruiting contracts guarantee the hire for one year. People just really don't know if this is the right job, right industry, right company, and if they can be successful there until a year in. I was lucky to negotiate only 3 month guarantees on many of my sales team hires, since there was more turn over in straight commission sales people, however most of my recruitment contracts over the years were for a one year guarantee.

I've always felt that you really haven't earned the right to walk away from something until you've proven to yourself that you can do it. Do it once, so you know you're not just giving up, and then after that, if you feel like it wasn't worth it, or you may have other fish to fry, then go for it. But for now, we're on week 7, and you're to throw more balls in the air.

Throwing more balls in the air!

So, we are dialing for dollars again! Re-read the earlier chapters, pull out your old notes on companies that you contacted to get the first job order. Hopefully, you have been good about data-basing all of your information, so you're not scrambling thru paperwork trying to find lists, the way that I did when I first started. Or who am I kidding, as I'm writing this book, I'm having to scramble thru old spirals and notebooks to find my notes. Ugh...to be organized is the best gift you can give yourself. It's taken me years to learn, but the sooner you spend the beginning and end of each day for organizing and planning the days ahead, the happier and more successful you'll be, so put those good habits to work now!

Balancing Act while Juggling

Eventually, the task of starting on a new job hunt, won't be so daunting. And there will come a day where clients call you, and you no longer have to be in this scenario so often. But this is where you cut your teeth as a recruiter. You are paying your dues, and learning everything from the ground up. Be sure to have fun at every step, making sure your days are managed between finding jobs, following up on the current jobs, finding candidates, data-basing, organizing, scheduling, and leaving open time to keep yourself organized!

For many years, 4pm was my "O" time! I have a TV in my office, which I don't recommend for everyone, especially the early years. But since I began video conferencing for clients back in 2000 before everyone was doing it, I already needed the TV, so only turned it on for the early news, and then back on again at 4pm to watch Oprah, and organize my calendar. Even if I had the mute button on while I organized and cleaned up notes and to-do's, it was a way to finish my day, and start an organized list for tomorrow's morning. I would rarely take calls at this time, unless it was very important. It was my time to hear myself think, and get me ready for my evening with my family. On the weekends, that "O" time which was used for Organizing & Oprah, ended up being a relaxation time before dinner...whether it was traditional tea time for myself to take a breath, or a cocktail hour start with my husband or with friends, the schedule of the day was important to keep to maintain good habits and enrich my life- for business and pleasure!

Before I close this chapter, I have to remind you that when all of this stuff your reading, especially here at week 7, sounds good in theory, but feels too hard to put into action- this is where you need to call your Mentor. This is what I prided myself on with recruiters I have trained, to basically get them thru the hump so they wouldn't give up. A little pep talk goes a long way, and if I didn't have those from other friends that were recruiting from home like I was, many of which many years older than me who became my mentors, more than friends- I don't think I would have been able to do it.

Those talks remind you that you're not alone in whatever you're feeling. Originally, I had been that mentor to many recruiters, but as you read this updated version of my training course, I'm not sure if I'll be able to speak one on one to you. I will have webinars and materials for review, but nothing beats a live person who has already done what you are trying to do.

As I write this book, I'm now looking for a literary agent to help me publish it. Why reinvent the wheel, when someone else can show you how to do it in a much better and faster way. Utilize the people that come to you in your life, and don't be afraid to seek them out. There are tons of people wanting to help you get to a better place. And then you will be passing those gifts forward later on too. It's a great place to be, and you need a mentor reminding you of how it's done, and to not give up!

Recruiters Emotional Intelligence

I think we touched upon the intuitiveness a Headhunting Housewife needs to do this job well. Learning to trust your instincts and gut feeling comes in very handy in this profession, and you need to be a good judge of character. Although I think we talked about this in the Client and Candidate chapters, I want to revisit this now to utilize your emotional intelligence with yourself, as you feel the 7 week itch, and may become anxious or nervous. In the same way you would empathize with a candidate or client, and often help "walk them off the ledge," so should you do this for yourself at times like this in your own life.

Being seven weeks into a new project, without a penny to show for your work doesn't come easy to many people. Lucky, being a mom, and wife, you're probably use to working very hard with little thanks, let alone money to prove your value! Luckily, with recruiting, the monetary reward is only weeks away, months at most. Just be sure to be patient with yourself, and keeping going, one step, and one week at a time. As I write these words, I'm thinking of someone I'm currently mentoring. We're only at about week three, and not even to week seven, but I could hear the doubts creep into his mind over an email, while requesting to re-schedule our call that week. I know that he had a very busy work week ahead, and understood, but he also mentioned a lunch he had with a successful recruiter friend. His friend went on to tell him that there was no way he could be a successful recruiter part-time. That the field was just too competitive for him to be successful, especially if he wasn't 100% invested in it, time-wise, yet.

I reminded him in a quick email that the best intentioned friends will often deter you from a new dream. I've seen this in my own life, and many others. Luckily, I was able to spout off a handful of real life examples contradicting his friend's comment. Luckily, one of my other students who was only a few weeks ahead in mentoring had just landed his first exclusive job order, while starting his recruiting business part time! Not to mention, many other success stories I could recount. This is why testimonials are so important, and one of the big reasons for this entire book. Where there's a will, there is always a way. I cannot wait for him to prove his friend wrong, as he continues on this journey!

In the same week, his email came over, I had another acquaintance who has called on me for recruiting advice in the past, call me for real estate advice. Similar to our friend above, she had just finished reading "Rich Dad, Poor Dad," and was excited to invest in some real estate. She was aware that I had a couple investment properties, and wanted my advice, and encouragement to move forward.

She also talked about a friend of hers trying to talk her out of investing in real estate because of the good old "I don't want to fix toilets at 2am" spiel. I've had rental properties for over seven years now, and have never fixed a thing. You can find people for that!! Anyway, I was happy to give her about 30 minutes of my own experience, covering legal docs to contractors to management companies to how to use Craigslist to find tenants! Even though I'm not a profession real estate investor, and usually don't offer advice in this realm- she just seemed to need the exact same thing most everyone needs when starting something new. She needed to be validated, told that she could do it too, and to be given enough tools and knowledge to be pointed in the right direction for her next steps. When the next obstacle comes up, as they always do, again, she'll simply need to push thru, and if a friendly voice that has done it before can help her move forward, than it's time well spent.

I give these examples to speak to your own emotional intelligence, and awareness of the negative feelings that will definitely stir inside you. You've felt these before in life, especially right before you embark on something really big and exciting, like a new career, new man, new house, new whatever.

Having a coach or mentor is often the peace of mind you can get thru the phone, or sometimes even thru a video clip, or words in a book, that keep you heading in the right direction. Try to do this for yourself as much as possible in life. And if you hit a wall, where you really feel like your wiggin out, just remember you're never alone. Anything you are trying to do, has been done before. I always find that a comforting thought. How much in life is really new? It's all been done before, for the most part. Someone else has already carved a path to get to the place you want to be. You just need to know what exactly that path is, and to make sure the destination is what you really want, and to find someone to help show you the way. Again, no need to reinvent the wheel, but you will have to reinvent yourself every so often so you can grow into new exciting things in life. Luckily, all the work you do now, will help to serve our daughters who are watching us close every day!

Week 7 Goal Checklist- Throw More Balls in Air

- ✓ Read Chapter 7
- ✓ Review Chapter 1-6 because your starting over
- ✓ As you work to close your first job order, continue cold call list
- ✓ Email mentor new client cold calls
- ✓ Do Not Get Discouraged- "It's the 7 Week Itch" It's only been 7 weeks- Typical learning curve takes 6 months when working it full time- persistence, persistence, persistence!!
- ✓ Maintain schedule making time for cold calling new clients
- ✓ Have systems in place: schedule, template emails, timelines

Chapter 8

WEEK 8: GET THE OFFER & CLOSE THE JOB

So, it's week 8, you've made it past the hump of Week 7, and you've thrown more balls in the air to the point that you're working a few jobs at once. With any luck, you will help push one of these jobs successfully to a close, which means an offer will be made and accepted. We'll discuss bringing that job to the close, as well as the other things you should be doing at this point in the process. I've attached a template for "Reference Checks" as you may be involved in this process too. And I have found it best to wait and check references until after the candidates has received the verbal offer. To think we are discussing offer letters and reference checking here in week 8 shows how far you have come! It's always interesting to me, how you can call someone one day in their car in the midst of going about their day, doing a job they have perhaps done for years, and your call changes the direction of their life potentially.

It's exciting to get to the final call with that candidate. You started out as strangers, yet you were a happy influence on their life. You called offering a better job with better pay and a chance for something new. How fun to call that sales rep early on who was earning $50k as a top rep at some company, and offer them a job where they would get $80k with an opportunity to earn six figures that first year. I always worked hiring for six figure opportunities only. It was interesting how some people would blow my call off, as if they didn't believe it, and others would welcome the call, and go on to make $500k on a job that I called them out of the blue.

My favorite story was quoted in Inc Magazine by one of our top producers for GE Medical. When I called her, I didn't realize this, but later she told the reporter that wrote the story. She said, "This woman, Diane O'Brien, called me out of the blue one day." And I'm paraphrasing here, as I don't remember the exact wording in the article, but she went on to say how she was bored out of her mind in her current job, and was only dreaming of something better, when my call came in. Her name was Gianna, she was a Lab Tech Director, and was working late in the lab that night, hating her job. It's a good thing she had an open mind to new opportunities, and took calls from strangers! Now, I will pat myself on the back in this story, as most recruiters would not call a lab tech for a sales job, but something in her background gave me a good gut feeling. Long story short, she became one of the best sales people, to go on to earn over ½ Million in a given year selling high end medical equipment for GE Medical.

I believe I have a lot of good karma still to come my way for all of the happy people I moved from one job to another. Starting off with a stranger on the phone. Then becoming friends for a couple months while the process worked its way out. Some were so sad not to get the job offer, but so many would get the job, and life would be better for them. I know that I was only a piece in a larger puzzle, but to be a change agent like that by connecting the right people at the right time, is thrilling. I happily did this for almost a decade before moving onto other ventures, as I've discussed. Yet, even in business development, and mentoring, I'm not on the front line anymore, but my work does result in the same effect. It's still fun, exciting, and enjoyable. It's good work. You are helping people find the right jobs, or helping them make the next big jump in their career, and to do it in a socially responsible industry like medical or clean technology is just the icing on the cake! Latley, IT has been a productive industry, so go where life takes you, when it feels right.

The Offer Letter

So, I've gone a bit long here on finally getting that offer, and the thrill of it all, even before you get the nice check in the mail. However, your job is not yet complete. The offer can bring up many issues that you will still have to mediate. Deals have fallen thru at the offer letter stage, some of which you cannot help, but I would bet the majority of failed offers comes from the recruiter not doing their due diligence during the process. Discussing non-competes in those early phone calls, reviewing compensation or commissions in further detail after a successful first interview. Making sure as the interviews near the final one, you are asking the right questions:

Have you discussed this with your spouse? How do they feel about this?

Would you be leaving anything on the table, money wise, or stock options that we should know about?

Do you have a non-compete? Discuss this.

Before the final interview, ask things like, If you were offered the job, would you take it?

What are your concerns about the job? Be sure to address any before the final interview.

Although many things can be done by email and text today, most of these important topics need to be discussed over the phone. Not only do you need to listen for all the stuff between the lines, but you also want to pick up on all the non-verbal pauses, or hesitations. It's not the yes or the no's, but how they say yes or no that gives away the truth of the matter...even if they don't know yet- you'll develop your sixth sense in knowing.

Closing the Deal

As a recruiter, your intuition becomes sharpened, and you learn the subtle cues. I was trained in six sigma process, and chronological in depth interviewing, as well as psychological profiling....all in the name of hiring better for clients, especially during my GE and Fusion days. And with all the training and ways to ask questions, it remained gaining the insights that come from what people don't say during an interview. Especially, the face to face interviews, where you get the benefit of seeing them up and close. This is why I only recommended Video Conferencing for middle interviews, the final ones always still need to be in person, in my opinion. There are too many subtle cues to pick up on. And your ability to understand these things will be the difference in you making hundreds of thousands of dollars as a recruiter, or not.

The better your ability to read people, and really listen to them. Not just to their words, but their pauses, or sighs, or body language. To watch their facial expressions when answering tough questions. To see their confidence, or lack thereof, these are the skill sets you'll master to become an excellent recruiter. Since we are on week eight, and in following the typical process, you would be closing a deal, you'll want to spend this time fine tuning how to do so.

You'll also find it funny how later, when you may be having drinks with clients after filling many positions, many managers seem to think you just sent them a resume, and weeks later they hired that person, and you got paid a lot more than that was worth. Smile, and don't take it personal. They don't always know all the behind the scenes work you do. They don't know how you reviewed hundreds of resumes, to give them that one great candidate. They don't know the phone calls you had before, during, or after the job offer that kept the process moving to a successful deal. And let's be honest, there are jobs I've closed, where I didn't have to work too hard. I've had times where one of the first people I called was the one! I felt it, and knew it, sent that person forward, who got the job, and I received the same amount of money as the person that took three months to get hired, with tons of phone calls and emails in-between. Your job with your client and candidate is to make it look easy. So, when they give you a wink as if you're robbing the bank, and not having to work too hard for all the money their company spends on recruiting, you can just smile, and don't say a word.

When Life Gets Messy

It's the same advice I give to my girlfriends in tough marriages. Save your bitching and complaining for your girlfriends- don't unload that stuff on your husband. They've already have had a tough day too, and it's too easy to try to blame someone, or try to sell your story, or prove "all the work you do."

I can say that most of my clients, as well as my husband, probably don't really get all the behind the scenes things I do to make something come out a success.

Now, they'll be the first to tell you if you're not performing well. If you have to hire 10 reps for a training class, and you're not sending good candidates which makes for a debacle, you'll hear it, and won't get paid. But if you make it happen, never apologize for the paycheck. I had trouble with this early on, and took less money than I was worth. Don't under estimate yourself. If anything, shoot higher. Whether a client paid me $10k or $40k for a fee, the job either got done, or it didn't. You've earned it, and if the position was filled on time, and everyone's happy, don't let anyone have you second guess yourself that you make too much.

Sometimes this can be similar to at home. I don't know what your home life is like, but I bet in general women are undervalued at home too. Hopefully not, but if you feel you are, take peace as you look around your home, and know that you helped build and run it. It's one thing for someone to take issue if your home is not running smooth, and you're not stocked with needed things, or you're dropping balls here and there. Then criticism may have a place to have you take a clearer look at things. Yet, if you sit in a well-organized, stocked home, that is clean and peaceful, with happy, healthy children getting good grades and being where they are supposed to be on time and who are also enjoying the ride- you've earned your pay day. At home, 'pay day' is knowing you are doing a good job because you can look around you and see it. Your quality of life improves with each passing year, and you can see your success thru a better lens, than just the paycheck of a job. Whether you've taken your headhunting dollars to create a magnificent home, or have treasured memories from trips you've paid for. Whatever the measure you use in the tangible sense, hopefully the happiness, security, and peace of mind this career gives you, will be evident in your home life.

In your career, you may not always know if you are doing well, until that pay check comes. I suppose that becomes more of the validation that the world is rewarding your efforts. But until that happens, or in life, with kids, or husband, or volunteering...any area where it's more important work but doesn't come with a pay check, don't lose sight of knowing where things really stand, and hold your own. Take pride in closing the deal, celebrate a job well done, and move on. And if you don't close that big job, luckily there's always another one around the corner, if that's what you really, really want. Take the lessons learned, and grow into a new and improved you!

Since I just left off on discussing taking pride in how you, as a mother, wife, and every other hat you wear, should take pride in doing it all so well, I need to put a disclaimer on this. I don't want you at week eight, to look around as you are putting all your time into this new business, which means laundry is piling up, and the bills are piling up, and you're out of milk....and think that you're a failure. Life does get messy. Even the best of us who are good at juggling life, have balls drop all over the place at times. And when you're starting a new venture, this is one of those times. However, like a good mentor would say to me, this is not normal or your base line. "Water always finds its level." Unlike the negative connotation of this quote used in old movies, he referenced this when seeking your own balance. You may have days where you are way off balance, or weeks and months where you feel that you are sinking, but you know where you typically settle. You know your own level, and what that looks like, so it's okay for the pendulum to swing crazy in one direction or the other at times. And times like starting something new, and creating a big change in your life, will often affect the peace and calm, or organization.

However, all I meant to get thru is that, at the end of this, you may end up at a new normal, or new level. Learning something new may throw off your balance for a while, but ideally, your new baseline will be even better. Maintain as much balance as you can thru your learning curve. Don't be hard on yourself when life gets messy, but do celebrate your life when all is good. That's worked for me, and something you should remember when it feels like things are falling apart. There not, they are just temporarily on the back burner.

Think of a room you need to organize- it always gets worse before it gets better. So, following that thinking, expect things to get a little messy at first, and have your families support and extra help at this time. Any time I start something new in my career, whether it was going from one a GE Sales Rep to a Pharmaceutical Rep, or from a recruiter to business owner, or to whatever. I've made sure my family, husband and kids included, were aware of a transition period. Mommy may need a little extra help when doing something that in the end, will benefit the entire family. Don't be afraid to ask for the support when needed, and even if you don't always get it, be easy on yourself, as other things may take second stage while you pursue this new path.

Reference Checks

I've attached a template a few pages ahead that gives some examples of Reference Check Questions. Many client companies will often want to do their own reference checks utilizing someone in HR, or even outsourcing this task to a third party. This way, they are sure to get an unbiased outcome.

When doing reference checks for a company, not too many ever went negative. Typically, if a candidate is giving you permission to call a list of references, they are usually going to say pretty nice things about this person. Once in a while, with good questions, you may hear a twinge of negativity or something that's off base, but that is pretty rare, and I don't recall ever having a candidate not get hired due to a bad reference check. Now, background checks are a bit different than reference checks, and are often outsourced by recruiting companies.

Background Checks

Background checks will confirm things like college degrees, driving records, and confirming other parts of the candidate's history, often including verifying dates of previous employment, maybe even w-2 information. Unlike reference checks, I can recall a couple situations where we were not able to hire someone who would have otherwise been hired due to a really bad driving record, or by lying about income or job information. Although I did reference checks thru out my headhunting career, I never performed my own background checks, and never offered this service. If asked by a client to cover these items, you can find a company to do it for you, and let the client know you would need to bill the cost incurred. Last time I checked, you could get a background check for under $100.

However, to make life easier, I would probably recommend steering clear of this, and leaving it to the client.

Week 8 Goal Checklist- Recruiting Balance

- ✓ Read Chapter 8
- ✓ Be sure your week equally balances your new work and your family!
- ✓ First month was a learning curve- maintain life balance...create your own schedule all inclusive.
- ✓ Follow gut- As you network thru clients and candidate- learn to trust gut instincts.
- ✓
- ✓ Continue recruiting basics while incorporating new insights.
- ✓ Work on getting new job order

Attachments:

Reference Check Template

Reference Check Examples from SalesSource:

2 Customers- Recent sales wins

Why did you go with Joe Shmoe on your last CT purchase?
Was this the first purchase from him? If not, how has he served you prior?
How would you rate Joe on a scale from 1-10?
What would you say is Joe's strongest characteristic as a sales rep?
What would you say is his weakest characteristic as a sales rep?
Would you continue to work with Joe even if he sold for a competitor or another company?

2 Prospects- Recent sales losses

Why didn't you go with Joe Shmoe on your last CT purchase?
Could he of done anything differently to win your business?
How would you rate Joe on a scale from 1-10?
What did you like about him during your interactions?
What did you perhaps not like so much when working with him?
Do you think you would buy from him in the future?

2 Peers- Sales Reps

How would you score Joe Schmoe on a scale from 1-10?
What are his strongest attributes?
Where has he ranked in your company?
Would you want to compete against him in a sales call?
What could he improve on?

Current Manager & Most Recent Manager

See Employment Ref form, but add following questions: How would you rate Joe on a scale from 1-10?
What was Joe's quota?
What did he achieve?

Where did he rank in your team?
Would you hire him again?

Inside-Sales Admin, Order Processor

Did you like working with Joe Schmoe?
Did you perceive him as a typical sales rep? How would you rate
Joe on a scale from 1-10?
Was he easy to get along with?
What did the rest of the company think of him?
Do you think he was successful?
Honestly, are you happy or sad to see him go?

Diane O'Brien

CHAPTER 9

WEEK 9: TOOLS OF TRADE

Database Basics

I have always found the concept of databases as an interesting topic since my first sales job in college. I have stocked many databases in many different ways thru my sales career. From a job I had selling advertising, where I would write contacts on index cards, the good old fashioned way, before inputting the data into a spreadsheet. To the sales jobs I had after college using my then 'palm pilot,' to later, more professional jobs, using GoldMine and ACT, and of course the good old Microsoft Access and good old Outlook.

I remember over the years feeling like a lot of the work I took time each day to save and enter into a 'system' didn't pay off. I always took care of current customers, and could keep those straight, but the time I would spend entering the basic contact info along with items like birthdays or how many kids, and their names only seemed to occasionally really pay off. Not to mention the fact that as years passed, the contact information would change, so just as I really built a great database- it already seemed out dated. Especially in the days when phone numbers changed often, and you couldn't keep your original cell phone number when you would switch companies. I remember years ago, when the commercial came on saying- you can now switch your service provider and keep your old number. Finally, a piece of contact info that might finally stay with my client, even when they move. That has been a very good thing for the world of recruiting and anyone trying to database contacts in general.

Of course, Murphy's Law in play, I saw this commercial days after I got a new cell phone and had to change my old favorite Manhattan number I used for years from my time working in the city. All these years later, my 917 area code phone number is still the only one that sticks in my mind better than all the other numbers I've had. 917-912-xxxx...I reluctantly changed phone service forfeiting my number, and it must have been days before that commercial came on! And being a sales girl, I would get a new cell phone number with each new sales company. Finally, in recent years, being able to keep numbers, it's nice to have a number on someone that never has to change, unless they move and want the local area code. If only emails did that as well, since those are still changing every few years for people as they change jobs and emails. The smarter candidates get a Gmail account, or a personal account that they keep even when they change Internet Service Providers (between Verizon or Comcast or whatever), or upon changing jobs.

Of course, it took me a while to figure this out. I remember years ago, when we needed to switch from Comcast to Verizon, actually keeping both in my house and almost paying double, as not to have to get rid of my Comcast email. Crazy, I know, but I knew as a recruiter, it was a big issue. And it was, not to mention Verizon having problems changing my work phone lines, and utilizing my business name in the caller id, which was important when running a busy recruiting business from home. Plus, if the power went out, I always had a backup service. Anyway, later, I learned to always keep my email thru a constant source as well.

So, sorry for the long story, but bottom line is that using a database now is easier than ever. Save the email, the cell phone, the zip code, name and title, and you're off to a great start!

How to use your Database

Now that you know what to put into your database, you want to be sure to form the correct habits of how to effectively utilize this resource. Every time you find a good resume, save it in the proper field. It won't take long to have a strong database of candidates. For example, you want to be able to email all of the medical sales reps in the Philadelphia region. You tag or mark all of these reps with a few clicks of the mouse, and you have a standard saved email for this opening that is then sent to every Philly rep you know within minutes. Because you also offer the finder fee, candidates will often send you good people they know, and your networking has begun within minutes of receiving your job order.

You'll get out as good as you give!

As you receive new resumes and hunt the job boards, always add the good resumes to your database religiously every day. You will do the same for clients you have- there will be far fewer clients in your database, but you will want to keep much more detailed information. Keep the job order saved in place of the resume, along with many personal notes on your contacts.

Be sure to be very diligent on the job specifics- You will probably feel like you're doing double work entering the info into the computer from your note pad after your phone call, but do it. As I mentioned before, thru all the years of working for different companies, or my own, I think I have tried every database software out there. File Maker, ACT, Access, Goldmine, Salesforce, Customized Outlook (favorite since I was lucky to have my IT expert Father customize buttons to quickly input info for contacts and create mass email lists), Bullhorn, and others. Bullhorn has been very effective for managing all the clients and emails. The company I currently consult for still uses Bullhorn, although they did add Outlook as the favorite for email in general.

If I were you, I'd start with Outlook, and just learn all the advanced options, so you can start making smart files from the beginning. Again, you want to remember the most important info, have info that you later will want to sort by. And notes you can quickly reference. Area Codes, Zip Codes, Cell Phone Numbers, Titles, Salary Range. Those are some of the basics, but the more you can add in, the better. Utilize LinkedIn to the fullest as well, as it will make your job much easier!

Networking Sites- Pro's and Con's

I should also take time to review all of the new social and professional networking sites popping up. LinkedIn today is my favorite, but if it wasn't for me reviewing notes I had written in training manuals years ago for new recruiters, I would have forgotten how my thinking has really changed and come a long way in fully embracing these sites. LinkedIn seemed to be the favorite among my colleagues, so I set up an account but didn't take too much time to truly network and add all of my contacts.

Early on, what concerned me was fear about the fact that they have access to all my contacts, and I don't take the time to read all of the fine print in their privacy policy or terms. I remember getting an email from someone asking me to join, and when I went on the site it became clear that just by signing up, and opening up your outlook contacts, they were sending mass emails out to people- who wants to do that? I recall becoming annoyed with those kinds of emails, and I definitely don't want to send those to clients, family or friends- or especially to old contacts that I should have deleted years ago.

I believe there was enough of a backlash on many of those type sites that they don't send those emails out anymore unless you give obvious approvals, but I would still be very careful with any of the new sites. I logged on to one recruiter friends site, and she had all her contacts 'open to the public.' If someone wanted to go after her clients, all the info was there on a platter- the name title, email, phone- information that would typically be guarded like gold in the old goldmine databases- and here it is for everyone to see.

Many recruiting companies do not even list client names or share companies they do business with, since recruiting is a very competitive business. They figure why let someone else know which companies are currently hiring. And there is also the thought that any of these 'free' online networking sites, can change at any time and go from free to a monthly charge. This happened to a new site we used with an old company. Not only did we spend time entering contacts into the system, but we even used it to score candidates and share comments. It may be fine for larger companies, but if you're a one man or one woman recruiter, or even a small recruiting firm with a few recruiters, I still think a secure customized system that is quick and easy to use is the best bet. After trying many, and listening to many recruiter friends in the industry at small and big companies alike, a simple system that you will actually use every day is what's needed.

Your system should be set up so you can quickly do mass emails to candidates you select in certain geographies. You want to be able to sort by city, zip code, area code, and/or industry. You could get more detailed entering salary and titles, but it's not necessary.

And remember, you really want to be saving the things that won't change much. Their name, number, city basically. And of course the copy of resume, but even that will need to be updated, so even though I keep a copy of the word resumes for quick references in my database- it's not necessary. I think once you get in the habit of entering all strong contacts religiously on a daily basis, then you can graduate to adding other categories you find useful- but start small, keeping it simple.

Now, it seems I've reviewed a lot of things to be cautious about, and as I mentioned a lot of those concerns were more prevalent when sites like LinkedIn and Facebook were new. Now, after they've worked out a lot of the quirks and kinks, I feel that the privacy risks are worth the reward. And as your professional life blends more with your personal life, work clients contacting me thru Facebook doesn't even bother me like it used to. I suppose we all go thru different stages of how we feel on new technology. Some of us embracing it right away, others taking longer. Some of us just being more private than others. Some of us being more paranoid or worried about what is done with all our private info. Today, with the IPhone I've been using for the past few years, I can tell you that I've hit "face time" by accident a couple times, and I don't want my face to pop up on a professional call by accident. Especially, if I'm in my gym, or walking around my backyard.

The older I get, the less I care. But, when starting a business, and you haven't proved your professionalism yet, you have to really watch how new clients may "perceive" you. Years ago, I used to be annoyed by someone washing dishes in the background while I was interviewing them. And then years later, when a CEO called me for a consulting gig, I found myself loading the dishwasher as he was interviewing me. So, it's all from perspective I suppose.

I went a bit off subject here from data basing information, but my point was that although the instant face time bothers me a bit now, I wouldn't be surprised if I used it all day long in a couple years. To think back in the year 2000, I had to install 3 ISDN lines into my home office to use a Polycom video conference equipment to conduct live interviews all day. And now, I can do a free Skype or Oovoo call, or use my IPhone to quickly see them live. And for free, when I paid (actually had the company I work for pay) for a $10k Polycom system and the $200 per interview price tag. Crazy how times have changed. And when you get perspective on how it used to be, just like thinking back to the FAX machine being obsolete. Everything can be Adobe scanned now, including signatures on contracts. I gave up my fax machine and number over 5 years ago. But 5 years prior to that, all my resumes were faxed to me before conducting interviews by an assistant, even though they were emailed as well. To think of the paper clutter my desk use to have is crazy.

So, all this new technology, or not so new anymore....is good. It's worth it. You can't really worry too much about competition taking clients. If they are happy with you, they are not going anywhere. Transparency in most areas does seem to be the best way for all involved. And the longer you take to embrace the new technology, the longer it may take you to build the network you need, or gain the credibility you'll need for a growing business.

Invoicing & Accounting Topic

Okay, I have to admit that out of this entire book discussing different topics, accounting is my least favorite. I'm not good at it, in fact, I really dislike dealing with numbers in general. I never minded doing a quick calculation on my calculator of what my commission would be on sale or a fee for placement. That's fun to quickly calculate how much you're going to make. But when it comes to tracking income, and expenses, and later the annual taxes. Uggh...the thought of it is not even good. After years of trying to figure it out every year, especially at tax time, I learned to get an accountant.

The good news is that I started forwarding all my info quarterly to an accountant to take care of it. The bad news was that one of my accountants years ago, did a pretty bad job, and instead of reviewing the work, I just signed on the dotted line, which ended up in an audit, which ended up in me paying out a big check at once. Not fun. Luckily, I'm a saver, so considering it must have been money I owed anyway, I wrote the check, and found another accountant. This one was better. I actually interviewed him like I would a candidate. The bad accountant was a referral from a friend believe it, or not. Usually, referrals are great, but it goes to show that you still shouldn't accept someone as an expert until you do your homework. I assumed a referral, and a Cornell graduate, knew what he was doing... but, not so much.

So, point being, find good people to help you as your business grows. I think many entrepreneurs love doing their business, but all those other hats are so annoying. Try to find other people to wear the other hats whenever possible, so you can do the parts you love. Accounting, and bookkeeping definitely fall under that category. The book, The E-Myth spoke in wise ways to this, and reminds all entrepreneurs what really happens as your dream of becoming a business owner takes affect!

As my life changed, so has my business over the years. Although for many years, I preferred being a 1099 thru my own company when consulting, the past few consulting gigs have turned into w-2 positions, when it made sense. Although, I like being an 'independent 1099' business, it's nice when you're an employee as a consultant, so you can have expenses paid, with a company credit card, and not worry about the bookkeeping of your own small business.

The down side of that, is that you are exclusive to them. That too can be good or bad. I like non-exclusivity in business, so I can consult for multiple CEO's or companies, at once. However working exclusively with one at a time, keeps life simpler. And remember, you can develop contracts that do not box you in, as you decide to grow your business. In recent years, I went from typical recruiting contracts with my clients, to Business Development recruiting contracts that I customized to fit what worked best for my lifestyle. I may be getting ahead of myself here, since we're focusing on headhunting and not business development. However, it's good for you to recognize that this career can grow in various ways, so that it can continue to suit your life and the lifestyle you desire as you grown and evolve.

Hiring Help

So, I just reviewed the need to hire good accountants. Some of those other areas that made sense for me to hire out, or outsource were IT help, sourcing for overflow of jobs, nanny, housekeeper, landscaper. Most of these hats, I did myself before getting crazy involved in my business. I knew from day one when my kids were young that a full time nanny was a necessity for me to be a successful mother and business owner.

If you have young kids at home, the best part of recruiting, is the ability to work from home. You, Moms out there, are the main reason I'm writing this book. It's to help anyone wanting to learn about headhunting. But, to think that so many moms rack their brain to find a good job they could do from home, but know nothing about the world of recruiting.

Recruiting would have never entered my radar, if it wasn't for my old boss, the CEO of Fusion Sales Partners, bringing this opportunity to me. Thanks Peter Groop! He built his company, and made his millions by empowering other people to do the same. He's created more entrepreneurs than anyone I personally know. I suppose developing an entrepreneurial mind set is even more important than teaching the technicalities of a job. Recruiting will be your business, but an entrepreneur is what you're evolving into. To create the life of your dreams. To live each day, the way you want to live it, while earning great money. To be in control of your time and life, you and whichever God you pray to! For all of you Mom's, it's not always an option to go work for a recruiting company in the corporate arena. There's no better way to learn a business than by watching someone else do the job every day. However, if I could learn an industry while sitting at a home office...a business I really knew nothing about prior to accepting the new role, then so can you. I found mentors, as I advise you to do. But other than weekly calls to my good friend and woman recruiter who had been recruiting for years, I was alone in figuring stuff out. And she was really more of an expert on the sourcing side (thanks Robin Holder in St. Louis!) When it came to developing good interviews, and reading resumes, and planning my travel calendar, and working with hiring managers, all that was learned on the job, from my home office.

You can do the same. You need the technical know-how, which you can find in a book, such as this one. And you need the entrepreneurial advice and inspiration from someone who's done it before, and can help guide you. That could be someone like me, or someone you find in your area, or on the internet. So, just like hiring out certain tasks to help you become a better person, or live a better life, don't forget there are a lot of people wanting to help you move up in the world. By hiring accountants, landscapers, housekeepers, nannies, IT help, or anything else, you are helping those people's business. There are people on the flip side, out there wanting to help you grow in your business, so be sure to find them.

This is something I speak a lot to young girls in college about, but it's just important to remember all thru your career. Even if you leave your career, and choose to be a stay at home mom. There will still be other women available to you, perhaps another mother, or neighbor, that can help inspire you, and lift you up to new levels.

You're going to be putting yourself out there in all kinds of new ways when starting this adventure. Remember to have courage, and be as much about helping others, as you hire help, as you are about helping yourself, as you work with mentors or other leaders that guide you.

Sourcing

I've spoken a lot on outsourcing tasks, and other than your nanny to help with kids and home, no one else is more important than a sourcing partner (if you choose to share your income), or a business partner (the biggest risk). A sourcing partner comes in very handy when you start to take on more openings than you can handle. If you land a 10 position contract, your excitement can quickly turn to fear when you realize it's too much work for you to handle. This is where a 'researcher' or 'sourcer' is important.

In the beginning, you'll want to learn how to find the candidates yourself, but if you're good at finding the job orders and getting them closed, it often makes sense for you to get help with the researching and reviewing of resumes. The bulk of people you need to review for any one given job is just too enormous for one person.

Now, if later, upon learning this business, you realize that you love the sourcing part, but not so much the client interaction, that's fine too. I have plenty of recruiter friends who make their living from home by simply filling the funnel with resumes to certain HR managers or other home based recruiters they split the fee with.

I've played all the roles, yet have found that I don't like the research as much as the "Biz Dev" or business development portion of the job. That's perhaps why my career choices have led me to end up focusing almost completely on the Biz Dev side, now being far removed from interviewing candidates at all anymore. However, for most of my life in this industry, I wore all hats, as you will in the beginning. Plus, it's good for you to understand from the beginning that both parts are important to placing a job. I know that my first CEO in the business put more value on my role as a strong interviewer and closer. So, he paid the researcher less money. However, when in my own business, although I started with the same mind set, I started doing full splits with sourcers. Especially when they could be taught to do full interviews, and speak directly to the clients as well. This freed up my time for things I enjoyed more, so it just made sense. Other sourcers, who simply sent resumes, would get only 25% of the final fee. And later, when consulting with other recruiting companies, they would take a 25% cut for the company name and expenses, etc. Too many cuts in the pie doesn't leave as much for you, but if your time becomes more important than the money, that may later suit you. However, in the beginning, and hopefully most of your career as a recruiter "working a desk," the more of those tasks you can do efficiently on your own, the better the reward. Having a big check, come in the mail, and getting to keep it all (except for taxes of course, and a % for charity off the top perhaps) is always a good thing.

Another thing I should mention here, is that when, and if you do decide to partner with a sourcer, a couple issues can come up. First, find one great sourcer that you can partner with and have a good working relationship with. You will be speaking to this person every day via the phone and email. You have to like that person. When I was looking for some new recruiting help, an old mentor of mine offered me his sourcer that he wasn't able to manage any longer. He assured me she was a good worker, and could do a great job. I interviewed her, but just didn't hit it off with her. Even if she did a great job, the thought of having to talk to her every day was not worth it. I can't remember if it was the tone of her voice, or some negative comments she made, but it just wasn't a match. Which is funny, because maybe like rentals, you shouldn't hire employees based on personal characteristics you like, just like I shouldn't buy a condo rental based on me liking it. It should maybe be on numbers alone like I always get told. Yet, for whatever reason, I just cannot go off the numbers alone- I have to feel it. That old mentor ended up keeping her as his main sourcer, and he would tease me how she made him over $100k the year I turned her down. Funny, and sad, but I would have still not have hired her. The daily interaction would have made me earn every penny of that money.

Similar to clients, as mentioned a few chapters ago. You may have to take on clients you don't like to land a contract, but I think you'll just be more successful if you focus on working with people you like. From sourcers, to clients, to CEO's.

Partners

The other positions I've discussed still have left you and you alone in the driver's seat. If you ever decide to take on a true 50/50 business partner, not just in sourcing, or one aspect of your business, but at true 50/50 partner in the entire business, be sure to give this one lots and lots of thought. As an advisor told me when I was considering taking on a partner, he said "Diane, this is like getting into bed with someone. Be sure you know and trust this person before you give away half your business!"

Now, for me, I did trust this person, and he was a trustworthy partner. He had helped me when I first started my recruiting business years prior, landing me one of my first exclusive and later retained contracts. So, it only seemed right when he was unexpectedly fired, and asked me about partnering with him in this recruiting business, did I say yes. It was more spontaneous than I would recommend ever making such a big decision. But sometimes, you just know. Sometimes, you just go with your gut. Which is what I've done most of my life in business and life, professionally and personally.

We had a great partnership for many years, landed huge accounts which maintained the six-figure level of income we were both wanting. When it was time for him to move on to other opportunities, we remained close friends. Even continuing as real estate partners in an investment property for many years later. I've been lucky to have good men and women come into my life. What's the saying? That some people come for a reason, some for a season, and some forever. Whichever it turns out to be, all relationships seem very worthwhile. And business relationships in particular are a good test of character, because it proves where your heart and head is at different times of life. Does money come first, or people? Obviously, we all say people, but until there's money on the line, not all of us choose that path.

Now, to further dive into why you would ever want to take on a partner, you have to think about the value it could add to your business. However, I say much of this with a grain of salt, since I don't always follow my best advice either. Another advisor told me that if you take on a business partner, make sure they bring opposite skill sets of your own. For instance, if one is good out in front of people, maybe the other should be good behind the scenes...the sales vs. operations idea. Yet, even in my own personal example, we were both the "sales." It made for great profits, but not so much long term business planning, and detail work.

In most cases however, you will be fine on your own. Maybe partnering somewhat with a recruiting sourcer as mentioned, but another business partner may not make sense unless you grow your business to the point of needing a lot more help. I'm talking about if you take on office space and hire a few employees. For all intents and purposes, that's not who I'm speaking to here. I'm talking to the Mom's out there...and the Dads who are at home wanting to have a nice, little simple business, and earn a nice simple low six figure income. If you do some splits, and only take on part of the recruiting role, you can still be home as a Mom or Dad, and earn around $60K. Less or more, depending upon how hard you want or need to work. This is the beauty of Recruiting. Not much startup cost, an industry that blankets thru all other industries, and people are always hiring. If you can grow and still keep it simple, without any partners involved, that usually the best, but see where it takes you, and what shows up in life, as you head down this path.

Cutting Edge Technology Backstory

Technology

Utilizing cutting edge technology help differentiate yourself from other recruiters. I did this when I became pregnant, and didn't want to fly all over the country to conduct interviews for my clients anymore. It was exciting for me as a single girl, but as a married woman with child on the way....not so much.

Video Conferencing was very new. In fact, I remember being pregnant with my first daughter and meeting the Polycom reps at their office to get all the information on how this video conferencing technology could work. Although I set out on this mission for personal reasons- wanting to keep my job without having to leave home as much, it ended up being life changing to our company. It's funny, looking back and remembering how I had to convince the CEO to let me install this in my home, and how it would save not only thousands in travel costs when meeting potential hires, but time savings for the managers that would often lose a week in the field because they were in some city for interviews. It was hugely successful, and we were able to make a record number of hires that year, and hit training deadline goals set forth by GE Medical, that we could have never have met prior to us utilizing video conferencing. When I left to start my own business, Fusion, the company I worked for, ended up installing 2 more systems in their corporate office. Even until a few years ago, when I started working in the Clean Tech industry, small recruiting companies that I would work and consult for were just starting to use this technology.

No wonder, I had an edge over the other home based recruiters. Technology was helping me get the jobs done faster and better. Business was booming, and could often do my job with PJ bottoms still on! Of course I had hair, makeup, and my business blazer on from the waste up, when video conferencing, but how cool to be so relaxed for interviews, and close more deals at the end of every month.

Video Conferencing at Home

There was the time I forgot to lock the camera movement which led to the person I was interviewing not only see my fluffy slippers, but saw my dog leaning his head on me to be petted while I did my professional interview! Funny times, but I got the job done, and client and candidates were happy. Also, if you choose to use Video Conferencing in today's market, technology has come a long way. You can still install the Polycom systems, but now there's Skype for free, there's companies like HireVue and TTI, which add another element to saving interviews for sharing. Do your research, and learn how to differentiate yourself in that market.

Now, separate from the technology differentiators, you want to focus on your brand. I know this sounds strange to my non marketing, or non-sales friends. But all good sales people know that the client is typically buying because of you more than the product. If they like you, they'll want to talk to you. Be personable, but always professional, and make it so that even when discussing business, you're cheerful and happy attitude comes thru. If we get to the core of everything, even cutting thru business, people want to be liked. They like the attention of people they think are similar, and are also "cool." They want to feel valued, and get a chance to "lighten up" whenever possible. People are way too serious in my opinion, so I do think it's important to be cheerful in this business. Most of the successful recruiters I've gotten to know share this quality, and in a good balance of playfulness, yet getting the job done. These are the people that enjoy charity events and conferences that may go late into the evening, but are up at the 8am meeting to discuss business goals.

Now, back to technology as part of your brand. Although the video conferencing like I mentioned, was cutting edge when I started using it in 2000, it's not so new anymore. Having said that, when I worked for a Clean Tech company back in 2008, they had just started utilizing that same system, and though it new. Another client from 2012 has yet to utilize video. So, I suppose it really all depends on where you fall on the technology curve. What's cutting edge to one, can be old school to another.

I can tell you that technology, and keeping up with it, this video conferencing as an example, has always helped differentiate me from the competition. To bring that new idea to my CEO to help hire quicker and cut costs really added a lot of value to me as a key contributor to the company. Past my role of recruiter or Director, it helped establish me as an idea person as well. And idea people are valued by CEO's. Always add value where you can with new ideas that improve the bottom line.

Even in areas where perhaps, the bottom line doesn't matter. I can think of two examples, where when in my own business, I wasn't even trying to gain a profit, but it just seemed like an interesting idea or technology that turned into something better than expected. How awesome in life when things turn out better than expected!

HireVue

One example is when I saw this small little start up called HireVue on the Oprah Winfrey show. I think this was back in 2007 or so? They were using software to do something similar to what I was doing with video conferencing in my recruiting business, yet they were able to record the interview, and have it sent to the candidate via mail. Basically, if you were going to be scheduled for a video conference, instead of myself sending you to a local office to conduct the interview, I could now send you HireVue's camera and software in the mail, and you could conduct the interview at your leisure. I tested this out myself first. And it was a very cool, unique, cutting edge technology.

I cannot remember the details of how it came to be, but somehow from my inquiry into HireVue about wanting to use their product, I must have spoken to the right person at the right time. A few weeks later, when they had a local ABC News reporter wanting to learn more about the product, they asked if I could be their spokesperson to show the reporter how HireVue helps the recruiting industry. Before I knew it, there was a news van in my driveway, and I was giving an interview in my office on the benefits of HireVue. Still love their name! Funny, I didn't think much of it at the time, but later, people were telling me they saw me on the news, and new clients came along.

I think my ideas on video conferencing, separate from my interviewing and recruiting experience, is what led a former CEO client to ask me to come to his office to be interviewed and photographed for INC magazine. The point being that you want to utilize new technology and let it differentiate you. Don't be afraid to just go out there, research it for yourself, call the owner, ask the right questions, and see what happens. It may help differentiate you as a recruiter, or simply gain you some good PR that you weren't expecting, but I don't think it can really ever hurt you. So, it's mostly upside.

Conferences

I think I've been to almost every major city in our country over the years, for either a live interview or conference, or trade show. When I was a sales girl representing GE Medical and Fusion Sales, it was always the McCormick Center in Chicago, year after year. I would quickly learn the fun evening events like the Corporate Sponsored parties at the Excalibur's, or Tavern On Rush's of the world, for each city. Separate from the formal Conferences, you will learn the early morning coffee shops, or cocktail bars that meetings take place in around each city. It's just as much fun to learn the culture of each city, similar to learning the culture of different companies you will hire for. San Francisco, (and they don't like being called San Fran!) has its own special vibe, and some of the coolest people I have yet to meet. Chicago, as mentioned is just pure fun, with their jazz bars and interesting mix. Boston always feels so smart with their Ivy League colleges, and large VC networks. NYC and DC go without mentioning. NYC is so cutting edge, and DC is so political. Palo Alto seems to have all the start-up junkies, and so many of the cities in between have a vibe that makes developing new business more of a pleasure, than a job. Sorry to go on, but how great is our country!

As you can see, a great fringe benefit of developing new business is the travel, if you get to the point you want to get out a bit more. It's funny how at certain times of my life, when my kids were young, travel was not desired by me much, and seen as an inconvenience. Then later, I was eager to get out a bit more, and go places again. For me, it's been in waves- whether it has to do with my kids ages, or just the ebb and flow of me wanting to be home more, or not.

It's so interesting how at one time, we can pray for one thing, and desire the exact opposite later in life. I remember after all the years working from home, how I prayed for my husband to have a job where he could be home too. It felt like having him here with me would be so fun, since the kids were in school all day, and we could have lunch together and have break times together. That's come true more lately, but when he first started working from home, and my wish seemed to come true....it was awful. It was too much time together and we wanted to kill each other. I actually purchased property in my small town to get out of the house. Later, I didn't need it, and enjoy being here with him again. But the travel monthly helped ease that as well. I think too much togetherness can sometimes be too much. And after the past 5 years of many annual conferences, I've been ready to pull back a little while again. I'm only scheduling ½ as many conferences these days, and typically make them warm places during the East Coast winter. The next step to keep things exciting may need to be international, so we'll see how that can come into play later? Separate from these conferences being a great place to have lots of face time with lots of different people, it's all the business cards you collect from meaningful conversations, and follow up with later that makes the difference.

It sounds easy, but it's not. Just like writing a book sounds relatively easy, but it's not. It's hard work. To shift thru the piles of business cards, usually bringing back hundreds from any given conference, your work just begins. You have to database them, LinkedIn with them, schedule calls to discuss recruiting needs. Later, as I became a business developer more than the actual recruiter, this also involved the right introduction at the right time to the right recruiter to take over the account...also not always an easy thing to do.

However, with a system in place, it works great. Every conference should net you new leads and contacts, which later turn into contracts! And if nothing else emerges regarding the client side, you have a lot more candidate contacts to pull from.

Now, keep in mind, if you're brand new to starting this recruiting business, you don't have to worry about going to conferences right away. I started my business with the phone and computer only for the first few years. Conferences have come in more handy when wanting to expand in different areas. Whether you want to find some new clients at a show near you, or if later you want to fly around to business develop for your own company, or one your consult for. This is an option, but not a necessity for a home based recruiter. Again, Headhunt from Home, or Headhunt in Heels...the choice is yours!

Week 9 Goal Checklist- Database & Tools of the Trade

- ✓ Read Chap 9
- ✓ Input all current clients into database
- ✓ Input all strong candidates into database
- ✓ Develop daily habit of inputting contacts into your database
- ✓ Review Accounting & Invoice Templates
- ✓ Review New Technologies for your business

Attachment-

Invoice Example

SalesSource Recruiting

□□□

INPUT ADDRESS

Phone 610-935-4858

dobrien@SalesSourceinc.com

INVOICE # 2011

.

October 31

XXX Capital, Inc.

Recruiting Services:

California Recruiting- Jennifer H.	$10,000.00
Texas Recruiting- Patrick M.	$ 10,000.00
Florida Recruiting- Retainer Fee	$ 2500.00
Georgia Recruiting- Retainer Fee	$ 2500.00
	$25,000.00

THANK YOU!

Payment is due upon receipt

Diane O'Brien

Chapter 10

WEEK 10: DIFFERENTIATE YOURSELF & LIFE BALANCE

Differentiate Yourself

Recruiters are a dime a dozen. Just like sales people, just like job orders. So how are you going to be any different from other "Tom, Dick or Sally" trying to recruit for company X? We spoke about many things that are important in previous chapters, like honesty, integrity, setting lower expectations while over delivering, etc. But what else? We covered honoring your client's time. Not making stupid mistakes that would keep the client from wanting to pick up the phone to speak with you when you call. Obviously, you need to be smart and intuitive in uncovering your client's true needs. Not just hearing what they are looking for as it may be written down on the job description, but really hearing what they are looking for in a person, and what makes someone a good fit for their company culture. Remember, you may have dozens of people on paper that can fit the job, but it will all come down to chemistry and culture, so that's what you need to figure out after you've crossed off the other checklist items.

Calibrating your search thru every phone conversation you have with the Hiring manager will get you closer to producing the right person that fits, and get the job done. You have to be a producer.

It's not quantity, but quality. Again, all cliché things we hear all the time, but you would be shocked how many recruiters just slam resumes hoping to get a hit. This is where you need to differentiate.

Differentiate Yourself thru Personal Touches

Hopefully, you get my point here, and just remember that above wanting to share information on the candidate- each call should be cheerful, simple, to the point, but light as well. Of course, depending on your audience. Some managers would love to laugh about things unrelated to business for 20 minutes if they had time, or others wanted straight talk quick. Learn your audience, and make each encounter a good one. That's the recipe to a long client relationship, and will differentiate you from the rest. To go deeper here, remember client's birthdays and Christmas cards and hand written thank you notes. These things go a long way and also help you differentiate. Christmas card memories make me smile, since me and an old business partner use to meet at a bar to sign Christmas cards, and one year, after drinking too much, we were writing too much, and our signatures went a bit crazy. I wouldn't recommend this, but it's funny how the clients that knew us well, who became our friends, had laughs about this for years. Even after I left the medical recruiting industry back in 2008, I remain friends with those same people, and still send them personal Christmas Cards.

Another item to differentiate yourself is to attend all the conferences and trade shows where people get to know you and recognize your name. Referrals go a long way, or a track record of success that someone hears about you from someone else, other than you, goes a long way too. LinkedIn came into effect more at the end of my "recruiting career". I remain on for my Biz Dev clients and for the companies I consult for, but to get referrals on the work that you do is priceless, so beef up your testimonials and referrals when you can.

From the very beginning, it's also very important when differentiating yourself, to view yourself as a recruiting partner and true consultant- not just a recruiter. I never really felt justified in this until I started earning retainers, but I wish I would have had the mind set when I started my business as a contingent recruiter. This is something I mentor a lot on now with contingent recruiters trying to land their first retained gig. I kind of feel like the feather that Dumbo was carrying as he flew. The feather has no real power, but it gave Dumbo the confidence he needed. More than teaching some basic skill sets you can find in a book, I find that mentoring a young recruiter, or even a young college grad is more about giving them the faith in their own power.

Corporate success, and your own recruiting success will just be material proof that you were strong at heart and made it happen thru sheer will when necessary. But regardless, remember to find a mentor who can make you feel invincible because I found those cheerleaders in my life, and they differentiated me and kept me balanced more than anything.

Differentiate Yourself using Technology

I spoke a lot to the great use of technology in the previous chapter, especially in ways it can help serve your business by making you faster and more productive. I should also mention it here again as a great differentiator when defining your value proposition, and how you differ from your competition. Re-visit the latest technologies, in the same way I used video technology, to give you an edge with your clients.

This could be thru new databases and customer management systems like a Bullhorn, or like utilizing new start-up ideas like HireVue was years ago, making it easier to interview candidates without flying to them. Oovoo is a new one I started using for mentoring calls, as I can now record them, which was more difficult to do on Skype. And recently TTI, "Take the Interview," has become a favorite video interviewing tool. Point being is to just keep up on new technologies that could help you succeed.

Differentiate Yourself thru Charity

This idea is truly charity based, from all of the conferences I have had to attend over the years. I have worked in many different industries over my career- Healthcare, IT, Clean Technology, among many others at this point. Many of the conferences, especially the ones GE put on were often connected to a charitable organization. Proceeds would be raised for a foundation while we got together to network thru a conference or golf outing, or whatever. This was also the case in Big Pharma, when I was a sales girl throwing lots of events for the doctors. Charities would often be attached in positive ways. Yet, I noticed when I joined the Clean Technology industry, and maybe this was because it is a newer industry...but none of the major annual conferences that I was attending were connected to any charities.

Now, a couple of the CEO's I got to know and respect, would connect Charitable Sponsorships thru their own companies. And even the two companies I worked, and consulted for, both Hobbs & Towne, and then Magellan Search Group. Neither seemed to have a lot of charitable stuff going on at that time. I ended up making charitable contributions part of my mission when I joined Magellan. I remember when I first started, I asked one of the Managers what they were doing charity wise? "Nothing, really," was the response. I thought this was a perfect opportunity to not only build out their business, but help a young company learn the benefits of giving back.

I asked the Conference leaders of a few of the large conferences in Clean-Tech about partnering with charities. The answer was also, "we're not really doing that." Although it was tough to re-direct the conferences agenda, I had better luck at the local level with client companies I could influence easier. Luckily, Magellan Search Group, which is run by very smart, young, innovative, and creative minds, took no time to answer that question very differently a year later. They instantly added charity event initiatives to the agenda to improve philanthropy within their organization. Emails started coming over with different runs, fundraisers, and charity balls that employees were getting involved in. They were following the CEO's new intention of being sure to "give back."

They didn't do it just for the good PR, they did it for the right reasons, and Magellan has been growing at a very fast rate. As I write these words, Magellan Search Group has become a highly socially responsible company. Having said this, that's a box I felt like I could quietly check. I'm not taking the credit, as I'm sure that young company would have gotten to that point without my influence on the CEO, or the management team. But I can say, that by making that a firm intention, and creating some new ideas of change, you can definitely jump start some ideas of good within the companies you recruit or consult for. It's another great benefit to being a recruiting consultant.

I'm still working on establishing a true charitable partnership between charities like Global Green USA, and the large Clean Tech Conferences. It takes time and effort, and although these things can often fall of the to-do list, a few small wins make the effort worthwhile. I was able to help land the President of Global Green, Matt Pedersen, a meeting with a colleague in Haiti while he was there with President Clinton's foundation after Katrina. They needed channels to get solar panels to the areas they were building schools, and I had a contact that could help facilitate that and lead them to other contacts. A small piece in a large puzzle, I know, but it felt good. A lot of emails, phone calls, and time, but I finally made the right connections to help a good cause. The president of Global Green USA did make sure to have the Communications Director call to thank me for what I had done to help, and it's always nice to be recognized for your hard work.

It was different than the thousands of dollars I would typically expect to roll in after such leg work, but it felt just as good, if not a little better. My point being is that whether the idea seeds and takes off, or withers on the vine- don't be afraid of utilizing new technology or even new thoughts to make things happen both in business, and for the greater good. In this case, I used both. The new idea to help Global Green, and the new social networking sites to connect the people who needed to be connected. It was like recruiting for a cause! Try it in your own business, as it feels great, and giving back does seem to benefit your bottom line in the long run anyway, as I'll write more about in the last chapter of "Life Balance."

Celebrating Success with Clients

Finally, in helping your clients remember that you are different than the other options out there. Be sure to recognize your successes with the client and make sure they are aware at the appropriate time. If you closed the job 2 weeks ahead of schedule, they may forget that in the long term. It's your job to be your own cheerleader to put that in report form, and be recognized for your accomplishments. Especially, when working with HR, you as an outside recruiter get forgotten. You may have hired 8 out of 10 people for a class, but the Hiring Manager may never know, or remember that they came from you, if you don't make them aware.

These are just a few ideas of how to differentiate yourself. I'll have to add to this more later, or in a follow up series, but for now, think on this, to figure out what will make you different. Think of how you can add value that no one else can. All of these ideas, turned action items, will help you sustain yourself as a recruiter for as long as you wish to do so.

Conferences for Business Development- "Headhunting in Heels"

Since I've been speaking a lot about the conferences I attend annually, let me explain a little more. There's a difference between

Trade Shows, and Conferences. Sometimes that line blurs, and you have a large trade show, along with conferences going on at the same time. Sometime, it's only a Conference, where it's all speakers, and networking parties. Usually, when I think of a trade show, I think of a large convention centers in the city lined with booths. I remember having to work the booth as a young sales girl at GE, and never really liked that much. As a recruiter, however, they became a good place to attend to get candidates and clients. Later, the conferences became a better source to find CEO's and other level C players that helped me on the business development side.

Basically, you want to utilize the right conferences in your market niche to source quality leads. A few great conversations with the right people can fuel your business and build relationships for years to come. In the beginning, you may only be developing new business, but later you can also use these annual conferences as a time to see old friends, and make face time with clients that have already helped build your business.

Life Balance

Now that we covered how you can continue to sustain yourself as a "Headhunting Housewife," we need to figure out how you're going to do all this and lead the happy family life too. After all, don't forget that the entire reason you probably bought this book, or looked me up on the internet was to find a way to do something you could be proud of, and make life better for you and your family.

I always like to start a new venture with the end in mind, since the middle can get so messy, we could forget where we started to go! Be sure when you start this adventure, and when you are jotting notes down of the goals you want to hit, starting with the numbers you want to make...be sure to add life style columns to that list also. When I first started my business, I didn't quite know enough to do this. After all, in college, and business, you are taught how to be a productive, hopefully wealthy, member of society, but not so much a socially responsible, and happy, healthy, productive member of society.

If you are not careful your goal of making $100k, will turn into $150K which will turn into $200K which will mean more help needed in the home, which could turn into a goal of $250K, which means help at work and home. Then it continues from there, and before you know it, you've gotten good at reaching monetary goals, but when you look out the window, your nanny is playing with your kids, instead of you! You hire extra help for everything else- someone to do the laundry, someone to pull the weeds, someone to cook dinner, and it all begins to be a lot to manage. Then, you invest your newly found profits into 2nd homes or investment properties, which ends up being more to manage.

More Maintenance and Management Time?

Of course you can always get property managers, but I'm just showing you a quick glimpse of how things can get out of control, if you're not careful. At some point, if you've hit most of your financial goals, but are still having no time to enjoy it with your family, then you really haven't done what you set out to do. And again, I'm speaking more to the ladies here, as I'm sure that sounds all good to most men. But as a woman, a mother, and a wife, I want to have the quality of life to enjoy all the things I've worked so hard for. I want a peaceful, quiet orderly home, that doesn't take multiple people in it to make it run. And to have enough left over to feel free from life's typical worries. I think most families would benefit more by investing extra money in another property or investment, to fuel their freedom! So, remember you have to decide these things. Maybe you do want that McMansion now if you could afford it? When that money does flow in, think how those changes may affect the kids, and your family? Would moving really add to their happiness, or are they better off staying in the home and community you raised them in?

If they are happy and thriving in your current home, neighborhood, and school, would you want to move, even if you could afford it? Or, maybe, your questions and answers at your stage of life can be different. Perhaps a bigger home would be great, or a new school district, or just a change of scenery that you can now afford. Maybe you have no children, which changes the game. Only you can ask these questions, and figure out the right answers. I would simply recommend asking yourself these questions, before the money rolls in. Similar to having a good exit strategy on a stock- it's much harder to see the answer when you're already in, and feeling the emotional charge. Ask and decide for yourself before the excitement begins!

What is enough?
Maybe you do want to take that original $100k goal and go for the $1M mark by expanding your small business to a few more

employees and office space? What would you have to give up making that a reality? What would you gain? Think how that type of commitment feels when you are responsible for other people's families. How would that affect you and your growing family? If you can think thru these scenarios, and not find out the hard way, you'll be happy you did! I strive to keep things as simple as possible. Simplicity is key. Finding your right number to make life great, and making it enough. Then just grow your fun time and quality of life without having to add to all the material stuff all the time.

Too many of us Americans work, work, work for more, more, more. Yet, I think there's a nice balance of having everything you want (materially anyway, as who can ever have enough experiences or trips to be satisfied!), and having all the time you want to enjoy it with the ones you love. We live summers at the beach when we want, we take the vacations when the kids are off school, and have dinner together almost every night. And most breakfasts. Much thanks goes to my amazing husband for being a great partner in this dream. This is happiness to me. Define your happiness, and make that the yardstick that you measure your success by, before the yardstick of money. Figure out how much money is needed to get there now, to help keep you guarded from the mindset that it's never enough. You can reach your "enough," especially as a recruiter, but not many recruiters reach happy, and reach their end game. Make sure you do, by having the right plan in mind from the start. This will ensure your own success, and ideally help guide the daughters you may have watching you!

For me, I think I slowed the pursuit of "wealth building" when my business made 3x times my expectations, but my happiness didn't grow 3x! In fact, quite the opposite. Life was just getting to be too much. I had taken on a business partner, and we had grown the Recruiting Business to include a Sales Team to manage for one of our Clients. Our bookkeeping had become a mess, which led to tax problems we had to solve the following year. Between my children growing too fast, and realizing there was more to life than working the desk, or managing people, I realized I had learned an important lesson. I changed course, made large business decisions, and set up a life that came to me in a dream one summer while sitting by the sea shore with my kids. Although, I dreamt up that dream over 5 years ago, it's only recently become my life. I wouldn't have the luxury of the time to sit and type these words if it wasn't for the changes I made. I'm also living a life that I hope to set as a better example for my two young girls, Madison and Morgan.

There were some decision points, where I knew what was financially better, but would not have been a good decision for my family. I'm embarrassed now to say how hard the choice was, as now, looking back 20/20, it should have been easy. But I had to learn the hard way at times. Luckily, if you start this venture with not only monetary goals, but life goals at the same time, you'll get to that great place of having all the money you need, as well as all the time you want to enjoy life with family and friends.

The most amazing lesson has been that whenever I've made the right decision, versus basing my decision on money gain or profit, it seems to always lead to more money down the road anyway. And looking back, when I've made the wrong decision, where money won over my heart or my gut feeling, that money always seemed to be short lived. Choose people over money every time, and you have to think of this from your client's perspective too. Good business shouldn't only benefit you, it should benefit everyone. You should get a very good value, but never rip someone off, even if they would blindly be willing to pay you more than what you thought your time was worth. And that number can only be decided by you. My time use to be valued in dollars. Now, my time is much more precious than a number. Of course, it takes more to motivate me these days, but some things are off the table completely, where that hasn't always been the case.

What will you decide? A client meeting that could generate $100k this year, or your daughters dance recital? Of course, you can rationalize either decision, and in many cases that $100k may help you make future recitals. But when years go by, and the money is winning, you've got 'capitalisitis.' A revamping of priorities will be needed!

Figure out what number is "enough", and although it's fine to grow goals, I believe there is a point where all remains balanced, and then a point where it tips- either towards career or family. Every family's number and time are different, so figure out what your happy number is and work backwards to get there. And when you find a way to make a lot more for no more time, you're in a very sweet spot.

Note to all Mom's

On the topic of life balance and figuring out how much is enough and how to spend your time. There's something that I learned from women that became my mentors, as well as thru thousands of interviews of women thru the years. I've found that many women, like to quit their jobs, if they can, and stay home with the kids, when they are young. Often, this means they need to go back to work around the time the children are near teen years, if not earlier.

I remember advice given to me by my recruiter friend, who was about 10 years ahead of me in life. She thought most women didn't really think that thru. It was often more of a short-term decision, than a long term plan. She said that most of her friends that wanted to stay home when the kids were very young, often had to return to work when the kids were getting near the teen years. The baby and toddler years are wonderful, and of course you don't want to miss those years. And luckily for you, if you become a "Headhunting Housewife," you won't have to choose. However, for most of the Mom's out there that don't have the luxury of being home the entire time, think about when it would be most important.

The toddler years are very important, as their learning the basics, and do need full attention, however if you can get help during this period, many great nannies, or daycares can help here, while the kids also get the benefit of socializing with other kids. I went the nanny route in my home, so I could have my recruiting business, but still be there to raise the kids as I wanted.

Yet, the teenage years, when the children near 12 thru college, is even more important, from what other Moms have said.   That's when you can't pay someone else to watch your kids, nor would you really want to. This is when they make the decisions that can affect their life for the rest of their lives. This is when they need to be driven around from activity to activity. I didn't mind the nanny doing the driving to Gymboree, dance, and playgroups, when they were toddlers, but as pre-teens, I sure to get a lot of information of what's going on in their lives. Not only from what they share with you, but also when your hear them to talk to friends during car pools. This is when you want to be around to help guide them. This is the time that may not be as fun or cute as helping the toddler, as helping a teenager takes a bit more strength. However, it does seem like this is a time you want to plan to be around. Originally, upon marrying, my plan was to stay home with the kids, however life happens, and thanks to the stock market disaster with the tech stocks in 2000, the year I was pregnant, that option was taken away from me early on.

So, originally, I just wanted to work enough to get home with the children, and live my original plan. As life would have it, as I continued to work, and enjoyed it, I no longer felt that "I had to" work, but "I wanted to," especially when I started my own business. Although, I could have financially stopped working and be home, I still wanted to expand our world, regarding homes, real estate, investments, college funds, etc, and not make my husband feel that he was doing it all on his own. Plus, he's a man that prefers me working, to keep the power balance, I suppose. Regardless, now that my kids are older, not only do I see what other women were talking about, as this is the time to be very present, as a Mom. As I'm getting older, I want to focus more and more on family. With the right priorities in place, work has simply become the icing on the cake of doing things that I love to do to help fuel the home life we've created.

I've been building our life for over 20 years now. I've proven what I needed to prove to myself regarding what I could do (and couldn't do) in Corporate America, and now is the time to start a new Chapter, literally! I want to have the balance that a work life provides, but I also want to be available as my little girls become young ladies. These are the years they are going to remember.

I'm only bringing this up, to make sure you have given thought to the long term plan with your kids. Again, if you are going to become a headhunter, you may not have to choose, and you can be around the entire time. Yet, ideally if you have to choose to really work hard at one point more than another, the earlier the better, in my opinion! Even if you decide to go work for a recruiting company for a few years before going out on your own. Do that first, so you can then be on your own schedule later. I hope that helps in some life planning ideas!

Create your Career

I'd like to speak more here to how to go about creating more partnerships with clients as you grow your recruiting business. Having the idea is just the start, but having faith and nurturing that seed into something real, is the trick. It's why CEO's are paid so much money, because not only can they have the vision, but they know how to commercialize that vision and turn it into money. And the good ones know exactly "what is enough" and how to exit smoothly and successfully. There is no reason you cannot follow their leads, and plan out where you want to go next, and help attract that very thing. Yes, this business, as life, may take on a path of its own, but usually if you have the big picture somewhat mapped out, it's amazing to see your dreams manifest into what you imagined.

For what is a business plan or proposal, other than your dream on paper. It makes it real, and helps crystallize an idea that's floating in your head. Simply looking at the larger career shifts I've made thru my career can attest to this. If you recall, I was a sales girl at Fusion selling for GE Medical when I started thinking of wanting to be home more in the future to start a family. I couldn't see how that was possible, as sales people are on the road in front of customers all day. But, that did not keep me from dreaming up something better, even if I couldn't see it clearly. Define as much of what you want as you can. Back then, I just wanted to make the same money, and still have fun talking to people, but do it from home more. Before I knew it, my CEO was calling me into his office to offer me a Recruiting Management position...that I could do from home!

Is this coincidence, or did I help attract this to me? Later, I found out from a colleague, that the CEO was first considering me for a Business Development role instead, to be a promotion from a sales girl. However, he hesitated on that position, since he knew I was at an age where kids were on the horizon, and recruiting may be a better fit. Another manager reminded him of that, and it's almost like other people were looking out for my self-interests, without me being aware. The one good thing I did was to take time really thinking about what I wanted, and I suppose I must have voiced that to colleagues, and that the rest took shape on its own.

From those early days, my dream of starting a business took hold, and starting that felt very lonely, and did feel like I was pushing a rock up-hill every day. But eventually, after months of persisting, contracts came in, and the dream was realized. I started my own recruiting business, became the small, home-grown, 'entrepreneur' that I wanted to be. I hit the numbers that would prove to me I was successful, and then new dreams were allowed to take hold.

Later, similar patterns continued, as I learn to trust this pattern. Not being afraid to dream up new, fun adventures within my business. That summer I discussed previously about wanting to maybe jump into a new industry, and thought about Clean Technology. How fortunate was it that Hobbs & Towne's headquarters were down the road from my home. I interviewed with all the partners, and was able to start as soon as I had hoped. And then as I valued my time more than money, I was able to negotiate "business development" deals where I would take a percentage of the contract I helped pull in, but wouldn't have to do any of the legwork. This too, could have only come into fruition by me thinking of a better ideal life. Not a better job, per se, but a better quality of life each year. Later, another company that I consulted and worked for, found me. The CEO liked my profile on LinkedIn and called me to offer a new, and better, Business Development position which continued to pay dividends. Those checks weren't always as large as some I've had before, but there's been nothing better than getting unexpected checks in the mail for contracts I no longer had "to work". Thank God I had the idea, and thank God it made for a very good value proposition for a young CEO. I much preferred finding an unexpected $5k in my mailbox for a contract I put together with a wind or solar company a year ago, versus a $10K check that I had to work all month to earn!

Again, my point here is to show real life examples. Even as I write this, how would I have ever imagined mentoring, or doing more charitable causes if I didn't stop to envision a better future. To always be thankful for what we have, but not afraid to go after something more. Especially, when the key priorities are in place and solid, like marriage, and kids. Then you have the freedom and are allowed the risk to go after whatever your heart can imagine. You will have failures, which will guide you to a better way, but keep dreaming up a better way. Have faith in this power for yourself as you carve out your next role in life. You may be starting out wanting to be a recruiter from home, but who knows where that can take you, as you learn to believe in yourself, and learn how to make your visions come true!

Week 10 Goal Checklist

Differentiate Yourself, and Congratulations on becoming a Headhunting Housewife!

- ✓ Read Chapter 10
- ✓ Congratulate yourself- you've completed the course- you know the recruiting basics.

- ✓ Determine what makes you different as a recruiter from all the others out there.

- ✓ How can you be different from the rest?
- ✓ What's your specialty?
- ✓ Have you developed any niche clients? If not, who are you going to focus on the next few weeks after you graduate the course?

Diane O'Brien